3 Day Getaways
Michigan Back Roads

by

Ron Rademacher

Have Fun
Ron

Revised Edition

Back Roads Publication
P.O. Box 168
Hart, Michigan 49420

PAGE NUMBER MAP

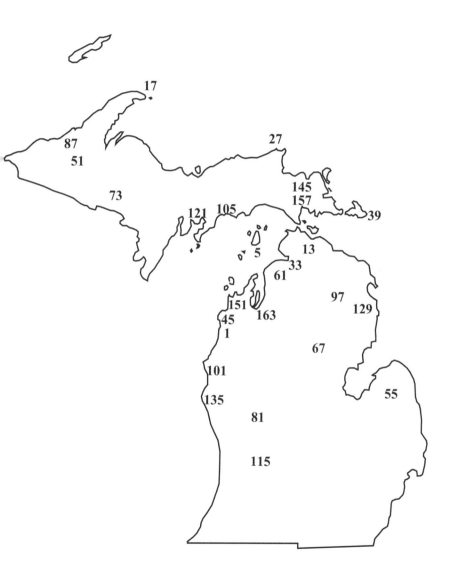

TABLE OF CONTENTS

Bear Lake Getaway 1

Beaver Island Getaway 5

Cheboygan Getaway 13

Copper Harbor Getaway 17

Crisp Point Lighthouse Getaway 27

Crooked River Getaway 33

Drummond Island Getaway 39

Frankfort Getaway 45

Ghost Light Getaway 51

Heart of the Thumb Getaway 55

Horton Creek Getaway 61

Houghton Lake Getaway 67

Iron County Getaway 73

Jugville Shack Getaway 81

The Konteka Getaway 87

Lewiston Getaway 97

Ludington Getaway 101

Manistique Getaway 105

Michigan Prairie Getaway 115

Nahma Getaway 121

Northern Sunrise Side Getaway 129

Pentwater Getaway 135

Port Huron Getaway 139

Sault Ste. Marie Getaway 145

Sleeping Bear Dune Getaway 151

St. Ignace Getaway 157

Timber Ridge Getaway 163

3 Day Getaways
Michigan Back Roads

by

Ron Rademacher

Back Roads Publication
P. O. Box 168
Hart, Michigan 49420

Acknowledgments

Cover Photograph – Crisp Point Lighthouse
Cover photograph by Ron Rademacher

Thanks are due to all the folks in the small Michigan towns who have made time for my presentations, endless questions and photographic intrusions.

Thanks to the lodging establishments and organizations who supported and sponsored this project.

A special thanks to Kathy Jacobs for the proof reading, a truly tedious job.

3 Day Getaways
Michigan Back Roads

by Ron Rademacher

Published by
Back Roads Publications
P. O. Box 168
Hart, Michigan 49420

Copyright © 2017 by Ron Rademacher

ISBN: 978-0-9883138-1-1

Bear Lake Getaway

The Bear Lake area is a favorite destination for nature lovers who want the quiet of a small town setting with access to a whole range of attractions and destinations. Bear Lake has the lake of course, but it has a whole lot more due to its proximity to the Manistee National Forest, Pere Marquette State Forest, Lake Michigan, the Manistee River and numerous historic and fun destinations. The whole northwest of Michigan can be explored from this little traveled and pristine area.

Day 1 - On The Water - Lakes and Rivers
You are within walking distance of ***Bear Lake*** itself. It is considered one of the best pan fish lakes in the entire area. The Betsie River to the north is excellent for easy canoeing and kayaking. If you are after Walleye, the nearby Manistee River flows over the Hodenpyl Dam and forms another reservoir at Wellston. While you are at it, the trail and foot bridge along the Hodenpyl will lead to a hidden waterfall. If it is sunbathing you are after, the inn has a pool and there is a marvelous tiny hidden beach on Lake Michigan just a few miles away at Pierport.

Day 2 - Historic Destinations - Bottle House - SS City of Milwaukee – Cabbage Shed
One of the most unique buildings in Michigan, the ***Bottle House*** in Kaleva, was the result of a happy accident. John Makinen operated a bottling plant in Kaleva, Michigan. The "happy accident" was simply, that he

noticed that soda pop in bottles stored in his warehouse didn't freeze during the cold northern Michigan winters. It was by this observation that he discovered the insulating properties of his bottles and, he had an idea. There just might be a use for the thousands of flawed and chipped bottles that were set aside during quality control inspections.

Mr. Makinen was an inventive man. He created a special cementing mixture that could be used to bind the bottles together into walls. With that process, he set about using more than 60,000 of his bottles to build his home which became known as the Bottle House. Being artistic as well as industrious, John Makinen wove different colored bottles into designs and words in the walls of the house including "Happy" on one side of the front door and "Home" on the other side. The Bottle House is the Historical Museum in Kaleva and is open in season for tours.

Anchored just off the road side north of Manistee, the car ferry, *SS City of Milwaukee,* makes for a most unique day trip and tour. In fact, this stop is great fun since the tour guides are very knowledgeable, making the history of the vessel and life on the Great Lakes come alive. After the Grand Trunk car ferry SS Milwaukee was lost with a crew of 52 men in an October 1929 storm, it was replaced by the SS City of Milwaukee. Built in 1931, the ferry operated for half a century hauling loaded rail cars across Lake Michigan. In fact, she could haul an entire train across the lake while passengers enjoyed the craftsman style accommodations above. Now a museum ship and a National Historic Landmark, the SS City of Milwaukee is the last unaltered example of a Great Lakes railroad car ferry. The museum complex includes a gift shop and a Coast Guard cutter that is also open for tours.

Highway 22 is the scenic drive along Lake Michigan with some of the most spectacular vistas the west coast of Michigan has to offer. As you drive along you may pass through Onekama, Michigan. At one time this town was the center of cabbage production in the state. A little way north is the town of Elberta and on the waterfront there is a place called the *Cabbage Shed*. It is a restaurant now, but it was the staging location for cabbages to be shipped to Chicago. The food is good, they know how to build a Guinness and it is rumored that they have had frozen cabbage bowling in the winter time.

Day 3 - Trails – North Country & Betsie Valley Trails The *North Country Trail* passes through the Manistee National Forest nearby. The *Betsie Valley Trail* showcases Michigan's natural splendor during a trip along the 22-miles created on the rails to trails project. Stretching north and west from Thompsonville to Frankfort, the crushed limestone and asphalt trail travels through Pere Marquette State Forest. Another option is the *Big M Trail Rail* that runs more than 18 miles with a surface that varies from dirt to grass to sand making it a favorite cross-country ski trail and a mountain bike trail. There are actually four segments, each with varying levels of difficulty, from easiest to most difficult.

Golf: There are 8 nice golf courses close to Bear Lake. Stay and play one course every day or mix in a little golf with the Morel Mushroom Festival at nearby Mesick in the spring.

Back Roads Lodging - The ***Bear Lake B & B*** offers modern amenities in one of the historic buildings in town. The B&B has a stunning Petoskey stone fireplace in the common area.

The ***Bear Lake Lodge*** offers modern comfortable lodgings in a motel setting.

Bear Lake B & B (may have closed – Covid)
www.bearlakebandb.com
231-864-2242

Bear Lake Lodge
231-864-3000

Beaver Island Getaway

Beaver Island, America's Emerald Isle, is full of history and mystery and is home to some of the most pristine natural wilderness anywhere in Michigan. Less developed than some other islands, the Beaver Island archipelago is remote and rustic without being primitive. Every amenity is at hand to reward the traveler who gets there.

Beaver Island, the largest island in Lake Michigan, is beautiful and has some of the most unique history anywhere in the state, including a one time King. Many peoples and nations have called this place home. Native Americans, stone circle builders, Mormon's, and the Irish have all made their mark here and those influences remain to this day. The trails, scenic drives, gorgeous bays and abundant wildlife make this island a cherished destination for nature lovers and those seeking a quiet getaway with a slower pace.

Day 1 - Downtown St. James - Mormon Print Shop - McDonoughs Market - Island Hardware - St. James Boat Shop

The main street follows the shore of Paradise Bay and the town itself brings to mind a New England fishing village. There are large signs posted along the street with details about the various peoples who inhabited the island and events that occurred here. One place that is a must visit is the old ***Mormon Print Shop*** which is now a museum. The colorful history of the island is preserved here. This is the place to learn all about James Jesse Strang who declared himself King 1850 and ruled his Mormon domain with an iron fist. He published the first newspaper in Northern Michigan and was elected to the legislature. Alas, he wasn't universally popular and was assassinated by two disgruntled followers. In addition to the story of King Strang, there are several other exhibits, some of which are rotated. Exhibits include early Irish life, Beaver Island musicians, Native American materials, and the "Then and Now" exhibit which depicts changes to the Island through pairs of matching photographs.

Along the main street you'll find two other museums, restaurants and shops. Shops are important if you plan to tour the nature areas of the island. *Mcdonoughs Market* is the place to get provisions for your getaway. They have fresh fruits, vegetables, fish and meat. Next door is the Dalwhinnie bakery and deli. *Island Hardware* is the place for all those hiking and exploring items and great gifts as well. Don't miss a visit to the *St. James Boat Shop*. There is a real artist building boats and paddle boards there. The workmanship is of the highest order. The island also has a friendly, well run Community Center that can supply maps, directions, and WiFi.

Day 2 - Natural Wonders - Birding Trail - Little Sand Bay - Millers Marsh

Nature lovers will have a busy time getting around to see everything the island has to offer. Many of the destinations on the island are in the wilderness on dirt roads or 2 track trails. Your getaway will be more enjoyable if you are prepared for the wilds of Michigan. Some folks bicycle all the way around the island. A few favorite sites are the Giant Birch Tree, Little Sand Bay, and the Birding Trail. There are seven lakes on the island. Each is worth a visit for photography, bird watching, and fishing.

The *Birding Trail* is well marked with signs and explanatory postings. There are more than 30 recommended viewing locations around the island. As the largest island in Lake Michigan, Beaver Island is a vital link in the chain of stopovers for migratory birds heading up-lake toward their northern breeding grounds. The Beaver Island Birding Trail is comprised of more than 12,000 acres of diverse habitats including prairie, cedar swamps, beaches, and hardwood forest. These provide ample sites for nesting. Typical of this diversity of habitat is *Little Sand Bay*. The preserve includes shrubs, cedar swamp, hardwoods and sand dunes, all accessible by a .4 mile pathway. The pathway to *Little Sand Bay* is augmented by boardwalks that allow visitors to pass through the area without disturbing the sensitive habitat.

Miller's Marsh is another favorite. This is a large nature preserve where you can see the work of some of the Beaver population, old growth trees, and sedges. It is said that in color tour season, photographers will wait for hours to capture the image of the trees reflected in the water.

Day 3 - Historic Sites - Protar's Tomb - Beaver Head Lighthouse

One day may not be enough if you are keen on history. Visit the cabin and tomb of ***Protar The Healer***. Feodor Protar, a scholar, actor, and publisher from Estonia emigrated to America. He came to Beaver Island in 1893. At that time there was no doctor on the island. Protar who was not a physician took on the role of healer, caring for patients and dispensing medicine until his death in 1925. His home and tomb are a few miles outside of town on Sloptown Rd. Due to his humanitarian work and selfless attention to the less fortunate, he became a beloved figure. He was known for his generosity in that he never required payment for his services from those who were impoverished, and he never discriminated. His home has been preserved and is open to visitors a few times each year. Note the enormous size of the cedar logs used in the construction of the cabin.

There are two lighthouses on Beaver Island. The St. James, or Whiskey Point Light, is on the northern end of the island. Whiskey Point was originally named for the 1838 fur trading post that operated on the point, and for the commodity that was the post's chief item of sale.

Beaver Head Lighthouse, atop a high bluff on the south end of the island, was built in 1858. It is open for visitors in the summer months and has items of historical significance on display. This light was a great aid to vessels working their way between Beaver Island and Gray's Reef. The view of Lake Michigan from the lantern room at the top of the 46-foot tower is unmatched.

In 1866, the attached yellow brick lighthouse keeper's dwelling was constructed. In 1915, the fog signal building was constructed. Other outbuildings on the grounds include an oil house, garage and storage building, and outhouse. A radio beacon was installed in 1962, at which time the lighthouse was decommissioned. The original Fourth Order Fresnel lens is on display in the keepers house.

The lighthouse is now run as the Beaver Island Lighthouse School and is available for students in northwest Michigan, aged sixteen to twenty-one, who have dropped out of school or are at risk of doing so. Part of the curriculum is to maintain the lighthouse and the other buildings on the site. Consequently, this lighthouse is in excellent condition.

Winter Fun – Many of the businesses on the island close for the winter. The trails are just great for snowshoes and hiking. Silent forests and pure air will make it a treat. There is lodging available in winter although getting there and back again can be sketchy if Lake Michigan decides to kick up her heels.

Along The Way - Giant Birch Tree - The "Plug" - Circle of Stones
There are lots of cool things hidden in the forests of Beaver Island. Some are just fun like the *Giant Birch Tree* - Just a short drive from town, this may be the biggest birch tree in Michigan. It is certainly a Champion Tree contender. Then a bit further along is another photo

spot. It is just a huge rock sticking up out of the ground. Islanders refer to it as "*The Plug*". Certainly the most enigmatic of the islands treasures would be the *Circle of Stones*. On the west side of Beaver Island below Angeline's Bluff is a circle of stones. The construction consists of a circle of glacial boulders that is nearly 400' feet across. Several of these stones have markings that have been interpreted as an ancient script, maps, and faces. A range of astronomical alignments have been identified and the center stone has a carved hole in the top When it was found in 1985, the area was isolated with the structure sitting in an open circular field surrounded by forest. An old two track road ran through the field and past Peshawbestown, an historic Native American village. Native American elders from Michigan, Wisconsin, and Ontario began to tell old tribal stories of a gathering place on the west side of Beaver Island which contained a stone calendar in the medicine wheel circle of life. The two track is now an improved gravel road, it seems that some stones were moved a bit, but the circle is there. It takes a bit of tramping around in the forest to get an idea of how big this is. There is another stone on the island that some say is a *carved face;* it sits in front of the Mormon Print Shop Museum.

Special Annual Events - Music is a part of daily life on the island. *Baroque on Beaver* is classical concert series and the *Beaver Island Music Festival* is one of a kind jam that is held every summer in a forest setting.
  Getting There - by Ferry in about 2 1/2 hours or *Island*

Airways can fly you there in about 20 minutes.

Back Roads Lodging - The *Erin Motel* is right on the water downtown.

Erin Motel – 231-448-2240

THERE

ARE

SEVEN

LIGHTHOUSES

TO

VISIT

NEAR

CHEBOYGAN

Cheboygan Getaway

While enjoying the unique shops along Main St. in downtown, you will be constantly reminded of the role waterways have played in the long history of this community. Lighthouses, museums, and the famous Cheboygan Opera House, are all within walking distance of the downtown parks.

If there is a boater's paradise, this may very well be it. Cheboygan is on the shore of Lake Huron within, sight of several islands, multiple lighthouses, the North Channel and this is the headwaters of the spectacular Inland Waterway. Cheboygan has been a home port for ferryboats to Bois Blanc Island, in the Straits of Mackinac, since 1890. The scenery around Cheboygan is fantastic in all four seasons.

Day 1 - Around Town

Of all of the historic structures in downtown Cheboygan, the *Opera House* is probably the most famous. Originally built in 1877, it hosted popular shows during the colorful lumbering era. Fires swept through the building in 1888 and again in 1903. In the mid 1960's the opera house closed its doors. The Cheboygan Area Arts Council got to work and in 1984 the elegantly restored Opera House again opened its doors. Acoustically, this Victorian theatre is considered superb. The décor is gorgeous, and the excellent shows have made this a major destination in the region. A tour will almost certainly be on your must do list, especially if you want to meet the ghost.

Home style cooking is always a favorite. "Alice's Restaurant" on Main Street, serves it up just the way Grandma used to. It is a good spot for a break while searching for those unusual antique shops that are hidden away.

Day 2 - Nature Day - Black Mountain Recreation Area - Ocqueoc Falls

Nature lovers can take a short drive to the ***Ocqueoc Waterfall*** near Onaway and hike the trail to the sinkholes. If you prefer to spend all day in a forested setting, the ***Black Mountain Recreation Area*** is just a few miles away. The network of trails is enormous with over 30 miles available for hiking, 60 miles for off road vehicles, and 80 groomed miles for snowmobiling. There are plenty of opportunities for other outdoor pursuits like camping, hunting, and fishing inside the recreation area, as well.

Day 3 - On the Water - Ferry Ride - Inland Waterway

If you prefer to stay close to town, a ***ferryboat ride*** to Bois Blanc Island may be just the thing or enjoy a couple of hours paddling a canoe on the Cheboygan River. For those planning a longer water excursion, the ***Inland Waterway*** is waiting for you. The Inland Waterway is Michigan's longest chain of rivers and lakes, allowing boaters to navigate from the mouth of the Cheboygan River 40 plus miles to Crooked Lake. The route is comprised of: Crooked Lake, Crooked River, Burt Lake,

Indian River, Mullet Lake, and the Cheboygan River. By leaving Lake Huron at the Cheboygan River, and following the inland waterway to Crooked Lake, Indians and fur traders had only a short portage to Little Traverse Bay thereby avoiding the treacherous Straits of Mackinac. This same historic water way is enjoyed today, in the summer months, by pleasure boaters. Many spend a weekend making the 87 mile round trip.

The route used by Indians and fur traders, also included Round Lake (near Lake Michigan), and a small stream from Round Lake to Crooked Lake, called Iduna Creek. This extension of naturally protected inland waters eliminated the dangerous journey around Waugoshance Point on Lake Michigan. It was possible to get from Petoskey to Cheboygan, without navigating the Northern Great Lakes. As many as 50 encampments used by various tribes have been documented along the course Inland Waterway.

Winter Fun - The Cheboygan area has more trails to explore than almost anywhere in Michigan. **North Eastern State Trail** is a favorite. This is a rail trail that runs 71 miles from Cheboygan to Alpena. You'll ride through silent pristine forests and across frozen lakes that stretch for miles. You can pause in villages and towns. You'll be treated to wildlife, and sunrises and sunsets. Cheboygan has the kind of lake effect snowfalls and winter storms that make for wondrous and magical winter recreation experiences. For the quiet winter sports, snowshoeing and crosscountry skiing, the ***Black***

Mountain Recreation Area is a favorite once again. There are trails that will delight the novice and challenge the more advanced.

Along The Way – Lighthouse Day – If you have an extra day or so, there are seven lighthouses or lighthouse ruins.

The *Cheboygan Crib Light* has been restored and is at the Doyle Recreation area at the mouth of the Cheboygan River.

The *River Front Range Light* is on the west side of the Cheboygan River just north of the drawbridge. It is being restored to its 1920's appearance.

The *Cheboygan Light* ruins are in Cheboygan State Park. The *Poe Reef Light* still has its black and white banded paint job. It is 2 miles offshore and can be viewed from the mouth of the river.

The *Fourteen Foot Shoal Light* with its distinctive red cast iron cap is nearly 2 miles offshore.

The *Spectacle Reef Light* stands 86 feet tall out in Lake Huron, about 11 miles east of the Straits of Mackinac. It is visible from the *Nine Mile Point Bed & Breakfast*.

The *Bois Blanc Island Light* is one of the oldest and was the 2nd lighthouse built on Lake Huron; it sits on the north side of the island and is now a private residence.

Back Roads Lodging - Sunrises, sunsets, starlit nights and the northern lights are all visible from the *Nine Mile Point B & B*.
www.ninemilepointbnb.com – 231-627-7870

Copper Harbor Getaway

Copper Harbor, spend just a few days there, and you will have a whole new understanding of what topography means. There is a big lake and sunsets and historic places, but it is the topography that steals the show, and the season doesn't matter either. This is an outdoors paradise, winter, spring, summer, and fall. There are shops, outfitters, breweries and some excellent places to eat, but they are there just so you can rest up and hit the outdoors again. Three days is hardly long enough. Fortunately, there are great lodging options, so you can stay another three days. There isn't any other place like Copper Harbor.

Copper brought early explorers to this remote location. While there isn't much mining activity, there are both modern mines and even some prehistoric mines, available for exploration. Most people who travel to Copper Harbor these days are interested in the wilderness and the outdoor activities. The scenery is incredible, the air is clear and pure, trees and water beckon from every direction. The town itself is small with only a few shops, but places like the *Old Country Store* still offer a huge variety of souvenirs, ice cream, and fudge.

The harbor was the port for copper shipments and the lighthouse is still there. Now the harbor is the site of one of the best July 4 fireworks displays anywhere. In addition to that, the ferry takes visitors out to Isle Royale by way of the harbor. In the warm months the harbor is a favorite for kayakers. In the winter, snowmobile riders make use of the broad expanse of open ice. On almost any night, the *Aurora Borealis* may appear, painting the sky above the harbor, with scintillating curtains of light.

Day 1 – Around Town

Copper Harbor is only a few blocks long, but there is a lot going on. Lake Superior and the harbor are just 2 blocks north of the main thoroughfare. Most of the shops, restaurants, and some of the lodging establishments are all in this compact area. It is easy to stroll all over town while planning a lighthouse boat tour or an easy hike on the breathtaking shoreline of *Hunter's Point Park*. A mile east is *Fort Wilkins State Park* and a sign marking the end of Route 41. The other end of Route 41 is at the southern tip of Florida. A half mile to the west is the beginning of the *Brockway Mountain Drive* and the *Copper Harbor Overlook*. The welcome center has the essential maps and guides needed for exploring those awesome trails and locating the incomparable scenic overlooks.

Day – 2 – Natural Wonders

Everywhere you look around Copper Harbor, natural wonders abound. From Lake Superior and Lake Medora, to the nearby waterfalls, to the abundant wildlife, visitors will find nature serving up something for every interest.

Of course, those northern lights can appear most any night. Here are some of favorites that should be on every list.

Estivant Pines – According to the brochures, the "Estivant Pines Sanctuary is a 377-acre stand of old growth Eastern White Pine growing in a mixed hardwood forest".

That is all true, but it hardly tells the story. This is a truly beautiful spot unlike anything else you will find. If you want to see virgin pines in a wilderness setting, this is the place. You will enter a world that for many is unknown. There are no improvements here and the going can be rugged. I am in good shape and these trails are a handful. If you go, dress properly and take water with you. This is a wild spot and you will want to stay for a while. I wouldn't recommend leaving the trail unless you are experienced and well equipped; rough terrain.

The primary loop is only a bit over a mile long. Deep in the forest the trail splits into two loops, the Memorial Grove Loop and the Cathedral Grove Loop. Ancient pines tower along both and each grove is worth exploring. Far inside is a swamp littered with giant fallen trees. This is a magical place and if you take your time and slow down, you will hear and sense things you have missed for a long, long time.

Hunter's Point Park is one of the real treasures in Copper Harbor. The point juts out into the harbor and is visible from downtown. There is excellent parking at the trail that gives access to the point and the Lake Superior shoreline. A handicap accessible boardwalk leads from the parking lot to a Lake Superior viewing deck. The trail on the point is a natural walking trail. There isn't much in the way of grooming. At several points along the way, side trails lead to the shoreline.

One option is to leave the trail and walk along the north shoreline of Lake Superior. The forests and lake views are spectacular. It is hard to believe that you are only a quarter mile from town. The unusual rock formations are volcanic in nature creating a wild scenic landscape. When a lake fog begins to roll in, the shoreline and forest take on a magical appearance. This is where you will take a lot of pictures.

Hunter's Point is a last stop for migrating birds before they cross Lake Superior on their way to Canada. Passerines by the thousands "line up" at the point and take flight in the early hours to make the trek across Lake Superior. Passerines are perching songbirds. What sets them apart from other songbirds is their feet which are designed to automatically grip and hang on to a perch. This allows them to roost in trees and sleep without falling to the ground.

Lake Fanny Hooe is just a couple of blocks from downtown and has a fishing pier and boat launch. Some say that the view of Lake Fanny Hooe from the Brockway Overlook, rivals that of the Lake of the Clouds. During color tour season it is not to be missed.

Raptor Migration - The spring migration of hawks and other raptors draws bird watchers from across the state. The Keweenaw Peninsula is a major route for migrating birds. Brockway Mountain and the Copper Harbor Overlook are also known as "hawk highway". From the overlook, the hawks and other raptors are sometimes at eye level. The Keweenaw's *Migratory Bird Festival* is held in Copper Harbor every year. It is a weekend full of great birding, presentations, bird walks and more.

Day – 3 – Unique Historic Destinations

There are mines, lighthouses and cemeteries to explore. Along with those, consider visiting these special places.

Fort Wilkins is a restored frontier army base. It was built in the 1800s to protect the port and harbor during the copper boom. The fort has been fully restored. On site reenactors bring the pioneer and mining days to life during the summer months. At the entrance to the Fort and the Campground is a road sign and map. The sign illustrates that this is the northern end of Route 41. The south end of that road is in Florida. These days everybody takes selfies there.

Isle Royale lies 50 miles away out in Lake Superior. This national treasure is still protected in near pristine condition. Hiking, backpacking and kayaking are popular as are the ancient copper pits that are scattered across the island. When planning a trip to the island, weather conditions are a major factor.

Day Trips

The ***Brockway Mountain Drive*** is really gorgeous. It is the highest paved road from the Rocky Mountains to the Allegheny Mountains. From the Copper Harbor Overlook, where you are more than 700 feet above the water, to the summit of West Bluff is less than 10 miles. Yet, it may be the most beautiful ride on the Keweenaw. If you plan to ride Brockway by bicycle, be prepared for some extremely steep hills. It really is a mountain. In addition, the winds can be very strong, but the scenic overlooks along the way from the Copper Harbor Overlook all the way out to West Bluff, make it all worth it. Conditions can be harsh out there even mighty oak trees are altered by the high winds. Trees of all kinds are stunted into dwarf Bonsai versions by the environment.

Eagle River Scenic Drive Route 26

As you leave Copper Harbor you are on Routes 41 & 26. Where those roads split you are confronted with a choice of which to take. It doesn't matter on which you decide, the back seat drivers will tell you to take the other, and we know that the back seat drivers are always right. In this case, everyone is right, both ways are wonderful. These roads make a loop at *Eagle River* so, whichever way you go, you can see it all and make your way back to Copper Harbor after a great day trip. Eagle River has a, waterfall, lighthouse, places to get food. On the way is the Jam Pot, down on Sand Bay. The Jam Pot is a shop run by monks and it may be the most expensive place to shop on the Keweenaw, good jam though.

There is more out there that is unique. Far out on the furthest point of the peninsula is the old rocket launch site. That is where Michigan first launched a rocket into space. There is the prehistoric *Delaware Mine* and the hidden *Cliff Cemetery*.

Trails

In addition to the trails at Hunter's Point and the Estivant Pines, hiking, biking, ATV, and snowmobile trails abound. Local outfitters have all the equipment and supplies. They and the visitors center have trail maps available.

The Keweenaw *ATV Trail System* is the largest in the state on private land. The *Mountain Bike Trail System* is Silver Rated. In England, it is considered the 7th best Mountain Bike Trail System in the United States.
Winter Fun

Winter transforms Copper Harbor into another kind of wonderland. The trails, lakes and forests are magnets for winter sports enthusiasts.

The Snowmobile Trail System, at 240 miles, is the largest in the State of Michigan. Brockway Mountain Drive closes during the winter months and becomes part of the snowmobile system. The system covers the entire peninsula and is for snowmobiles only.

Mount Bohemia Ski Hill at Lac La Belle, Michigan has first class facilities. One unique feature is the shuttle bus. The bus is equipped with a sound system, however, the only music that is played is music by ABBA. I would go just to ride that bus and listen to ABBA.

CopperDog 150 Sled Dog Race – Usually held the first weekend in March, CopperDog is actually two sled dog races, CopperDog 150 and CopperDog 40. CopperDog 150 covers 150 miles in three days with teams of ten dogs competing. Between the two races there are more than 350 dogs racing through the Keweenaw Peninsula every March. Mushers come from around the world for this event. Americans and Canadians are there. In a couple of the races, a musher from South Africa was in the race.

Lodging

Three days is hardly enough to explore all there is to enjoy around Copper Harbor. Two of the lodging establishments sponsored and supported this work. *The Pines* and *Mariner North* are both excellent lodging options and both serve great food in their restaurants. Planning ahead is important for a visit to Copper Harbor. Visitors come for extended stays, in fact, 60% - 70% of those traveling here are from out of state. Extending your stay may be necessary to get even part of these done.

THE

CRISP POINT

LIGHTHOUSE

IS

THE

REMOTEST

FUNCTIONING

LIGHTHOUSE

IN

MICHIGAN

Crisp Point Lighthouse Getaway

The Crisp Point Lighthouse, between the mouth of the Two Hearted River and Whitefish Point, has been helping protect traffic on Lake Superior since 1904. The original plot of land was 15 acres and was purchased for $30.00. The original tower was 58 feet tall topped off with a fourth order red Fresnel lens. The lighthouse was badly needed. This stretch of coastline was known as the "Shipwreck Coast". Lake Superior claimed many victims here; the most famous being the Edmund Fitzgerald. The "Major" and the "William Nottingham" are other notable ships wrecked near the point. The area was dangerous for land-based structures too. The Crisp Point Lighthouse was once on the Lighthouse Digest Magazine most endangered lighthouse list for the Unites States.

For those intent on visiting as many Great Lakes lighthouses as possible, the Crisp Point Lighthouse is a high priority. For some it is a major entry on their "bucket list". Part of the allure of this particular lighthouse is the incredible beauty of the setting. Another feature is the remote location. By some accounts the Crisp Point Lighthouse is the remotest operating light on the mainland. The word remote about sums it up, but with a little planning, Crisp Point is surprisingly easy to visit. After a long drive on a gravel road there it is, perched on the shore of Lake Superior. It takes some time to drive there, but not so far that it isn't great for a day trip. After leaving the paved road, it is only about an hour of well-marked gravel roads and, those roads traverse beautiful forests and serve up stunning views of Lake Superior along the way.

Upon arrival, the short walk from the parking area to the lighthouse and visitors center is a pleasant change. After all, the drive to the point involves many miles of very rough and dusty roads through the wilderness. The going is slow, but Crisp Point will make you forget all about it. This is on the shore of Lake Superior, so there is sand and dunes and rocks, but there is also an excellent system of boardwalks so access to the light and the lake is easy.

When the lake and shoreline come into view, one can almost forget the lighthouse was the purpose of the trip. The sheer beauty of the scene challenges description. The rocky shoreline stretches endlessly in both directions. Old pilings and huge rocks are visible near the shore. At times a giant freighter, or "laker" will be visible far out on the horizon where the sky meets Lake Superior. If you pause on one of the benches to just drink it all in, you will slowly realize that the only sounds are waves slapping the shore, wind in the trees, birdsong and laughter. This place is so magical, you will be glad you planned to spend a lot of time here.

After daydreaming and gazing at the water there is fun to be had if you know where to look. It is a good idea to check out the visitor's Center. Dedicated volunteers from the Crisp Point Historical Society are on hand with answers to questions and a wealth of historical information about the light. They can tell you about climbing the tower, about the pilings in the lake and where the best rock collecting is including, agates and "yooperlites", the stones that glow in the dark.

Then it is time to hit the beach. There are so many things to take pictures of it can be overwhelming. The beach is beautiful, and the lake scenery is everchanging. On the day I climbed to the top of the lighthouse the air was clear when I started up. Within a few minutes of reaching the top a fog bank began to roll in. First it obscured a ship far out on the water, then it engulfed the lighthouse and then the beach. Things kept changing. Within a short time, the fog burned off and the sun shone through again. I took a hundred pictures that day. Heck, I took 20 pictures of the rocks we were picking up. Yep, this is a rock-hound paradise.

OTHER ATTRACTIONS - So, since the lighthouse is easy to visit, there will probably be time to check out some of the other outstanding attractions in the area. Just outside of Paradise, Tahquamenon Falls is the most famous attraction in the region and is said to be one of the most photographed waterfalls in the world. If you happen to be traveling to the lighthouse from Pine Stump Junction, you will go right by the mouth of the Two Hearted River. There is a rustic campground there and a suspension footbridge out to the beach. The scenery there is breathtakingly beautiful. Within a reasonable drive can be found Whitefish Point, Deer Park and old Seney. One destination that is often overlooked is the Lumber Museum in Newberry. The exhibits bring the lumber era to life and some of the objects on display are like none I have ever seen anywhere. The historic photographs on the walls are worth the trip all by themselves. Our friends at the lighthouse or at the Halfway Lake Cottages in Newberry can provide directions, current road conditions and some ideas on other nearby attractions.

GETTING LOST - The stories told of people getting lost are true. In 1928 while deer hunting in the Big Tahquamenon Falls area in a large swamp, Roy Singleton found a man lost and took him to Crisp Point where the Singleton family was living. This man was Lou Williams from Ohio, known as the "Buckeye Poet". Mr. Williams had been lost for three days when Roy found him at dusk the third night.

In modern times travelers get lost on old logging roads trying to make their way from Tahquamenon Falls to the lighthouse following the GPS in a car. Just a few years ago, two women attempted to get to the light via GPS. They became stranded for several days and had to sustain themselves with girl scout cookies. They did have the right idea on supplies. Take what you will need for your day trip to the lighthouse, there are no convenience stores, no gas stations.

DIRECTIONS – There is a lot to discover near Crisp Point, however it cannot be emphasized enough that this is a wilderness area. Cell phone service can be sketchy, and GPS can be downright unreliable. On a map it looks easy, Tahquamenon Falls and the Lighthouse are only a few miles apart. Don't be fooled, it is easy to get lost unless, you follow the directions offered by the Lighthouse Association on their website. Basically, the main road between Paradise and Newberry is M-123. Midway on that paved road you will find Route 500 which is gravel. Route 500 may be rough, but it will get you to the light quickly and safely. If you are west near Pine Stump Junction on Route H-37, you can take the road heading east to the lighthouse.

IMPORTANT INFORMATION

Crisp Point Lighthouse Historical Society website
www.crisppointlighthouse.org.
The lighthouse grounds are always open. Quiet hours are from 11 PM to 6 AM. Lighthouse and Visitor Center (including bathrooms) are closed during the winter. Emergency phone is available all year. No camping.

LODGINGS

Chris & Julie Wahl
Halfway Lake Cottages
16878 County Road 505
Newberry, MI. 49868
906-869-0098
www.halfwaylake.com.

THE

INLAND

WATERWAY

MUSEUM

IS

IN

ALANSON

Crooked River Getaway

The Crooked River connects Crooked Lake to Burt Lake, as the waters of the Inland Waterway, flow toward distant Lake Huron. The waterway drops two feet at the Crooked River Lock in Alanson. Alanson, with its quaint swinging bridge, Hillside Gardens, Inland Waterway Museum, and **Stafford's Crooked River Lodge**, is a beautiful spot, from which to explore the northeast on a Michigan 3 Day Getaway. The Crooked River lives up to its name, with picturesque spots like the Devil's Elbow and the Oxbow. Visitors in kayaks and canoes will often encounter deer, herons, and other wildlife on the waterway. Boaters can go on a color tour on the Inland Water Way, and cruise Maple Bay and Burt Lake.

Day 1 - Around Town - Inland Waterway Museum - Hillside Gardens - Railroad Depot
The Inland Water Way is a series of lakes and rivers, with a few portages, that connects Lake Huron to Lake Michigan. The **Inland Water Route Historical Museum,** in downtown Alanson, brings the stories and legends of this historic waterway to life. The museum displays photos and artifacts from each community along the entire water route; Conway, Oden, Ponshewaing, Alanson, Indian River, Topinabee, and Cheboygan. The museum also includes displays on logging, railroad use, and lodging. Each was pivotal to the development of Northern Michigan.

Across the street from the museum, is the old **Railroad Depot**. The Alanson Depot dates back to the 1880s when Northern Michigan was mostly wilderness. Then the lumber industry took off, and the railroads boomed. The line through Alanson to Mackinaw City opened in 1883. After the forests were gone, tourism was the next opportunity, and this part of the railroad became known as "The Fishing Line". The Depot is now a favorite local dining spot. They have dozens of photos on the walls depicting the colorful characters and events that helped the area grow.

Another unique feature in Alanson, is the area known as the **Hillside Gardens**. Whether out for a stroll or driving through, you can't miss the extensive flower beds right on the main thoroughfare. In 1979, a small group of volunteers got together and acquired the property. They have planted and maintained the hillside gardens ever since. The area has become a favorite spot for crafters and gardeners to gather.

Day 2 - Scenic Drive - Tunnel of Trees - Good Hart General Store - 100 Steps Gorge
A full day of discovery and fun begins with a short drive north out of Alanson on Route 31. Less than 10 miles north is the small community of Pellston. Here we turn right or east on Route C-64. This is a beautiful drive through wooded hills. In a few miles the area becomes a Biological Station established by the University of Michigan. Keep alert for a small turn off on the south side of the road marked by a sign and split rail fences.

This is the parking area for the ***100 Steps Gorge***. Locally known as "Big Springs", it is missed by most motorists. This is a great stop to see rare beauty and build an appetite for later.

The name 100 Steps is appropriate. At the edge of the parking area, steps begin the descent into the canyon. There are 100 steps, and the way is very steep, but it is worth it. At the bottom is a pristine forest and pure running streams. The streams are formed by springs that bubble right out of the hillside. An interesting phenomenon occurs here. There is a 10 - 15 degree temperature change, from the top of the steps to the bottom. Even in winter it is several degrees cooler at the bottom of the steps, than it is at the top. When the climb to the top is completed, return to Pellston, turn north again to Route C-66 and turn west to find Cross Village. Visitors from all over the world, take the scenic drive, through the ***Tunnel of Trees***. The drive is Route 119 along Lake Michigan Cross Village is at the north end, where the famous Legs Inn can be found with its awesome views of Lake Michigan. Harbor Springs is at the south end. The roadway is narrow and winds through the trees which form a roof over the road to create the "tunnel". The Legs Inn, open in summer, is a favorite stopping place for bikers. Cool drinks are available, and the restaurant specializes in Polish dishes.

As you follow the road south, there are bent trees, that mark the old Indian trail. Signs mark some of the ancient meeting places. ***Thorn Swift Nature Preserve*** offers easy hiking trails to the lake, and an interpretive center.

Day 3 - Petoskey - Petoskey Stones - Stafford's Art Gallery - Urban Waterfall

In the upper peninsula, rock hounds go looking for agates. In northwest Michigan, the most sought after treasure, is the *Petoskey Stone*, the state stone of Michigan. Unpolished they don't look like much, just another bit of fossilized coral, but when polished, the unique beauty of these stones comes shining through. Their appearance is so captivating that Petoskey Stones have be used for everything from coasters to jewelry. We won't run out of them as long as we have winters. The movement of ice, against the sand of the lake shore, stirs up new stones every spring at the water's edge. The name comes from an Ottawa Indian, Chief Pet-O-Sega. The city of Petoskey, Michigan, is also named after him, and is the center of the area, where the stones are found on the beaches and sand dunes.

Excellent examples of finished Petoskey Stones can be found at *Stafford's Gallery* on Rose Street, in downtown Petoskey. This is generally regarded as the best gallery and gift shop, in a town that is known for its shops and galleries. On the same property, is the historic *Perry Hotel,* with its famous eateries.

While exploring the town, you may want to visit the museum that is across the main road from the shopping district. Directly opposite the museum is a small park with a man-made *urban waterfall*. This spot is also at one end of an improved trail, that winds along the river, all the way to the other side of town.

Winter Fun - Just across the road from Stafford's Crooked River Lodge in Alanson, is a trail head, giving access to hundreds of miles of snowmobile trails. You can sled all the way to Indian River, Harbor Springs, or Mackinaw City. Of course, there are also cross country ski trails right from the lodge property.

Along The Way - Dark Sky Park - Bliss Fest
There are only a few Dark Sky Parks in the United States. The *Headlands International Dark Sky Park,* is in the extreme northwest corner of Emmet County. Dark Sky Parks are protected lands, that possess exceptionally starry night skies. Headlands is 600 acres of old growth forest, with more than 4 miles of trails. This park includes more than two miles of Lake Michigan shoreline, where 80+ ships have wrecked. The shoreline is a great place to see the northern lights. There is also a self-guided cell phone tour. From Alanson go north on 31 to Carp Lake. Go west to Route C-81 and go north to Cecil Bay. Watch for W. Central Ave. Go west and be aware that some of the roads may be a bit rough.
If you are in the area at the right time of year, music lovers gather for *Bliss Fest*. They have been celebrating music, dance and song writing for more than three decades. The festival takes place in Bliss, Michigan. Contact their website for schedules.

Back Roads Lodging - At *Stafford's Crooked River Lodge* in Alanson. Don't miss their on-site trails and parks. www.staffords.com 231-548-5000

DRUMMOND

ISLAND

IS

FAMOUS

IT'S

MILES

OF

CHALLENGING

ORV

TRAILS

Drummond Island Getaway

Off the eastern end of Michigan's Upper Peninsula, lies the "Gem of Lake Huron", Drummond Island. Any destination can be described as "unique", but this hidden treasure really is a unique paradise. Even the short list is impressive; 150 miles of shoreline, 30 bays and coves, 34 inland lakes (ooh fishing), 100 miles of ORV trails, comprising one of the largest closed loop trail systems for off road - ATV / ORV exploration in the U.S. There are 70 miles of groomed snowmobile trails, more than a dozen shipwrecks, 58 neighboring islands, a lighthouse, and a ferry ride.

Beyond the short list, there are the championship golf courses, loads of hiking and birding trails, there is even one called the Rainbow Trail. The Maxton Plains are home to a rare alvar formation, perhaps the largest in the world, and then, there are the fossil ledges. On top of all this, the Harbor Island National Wildlife Refuge, is just across the way. The history of the island goes back centuries, and is preserved at the Historical Museum. Unusual shops, great places to eat, and a whole range of lodging choices, combine to ensure that this is a 3 Day Michigan Getaway that will have you coming back season after season.

Day -1- Ferry Ride – The ferry ride to the island, affords a great view of the ***DeTour Reef Lighthouse,*** which marks the mouth of the St. Mary's River. The lighthouse was originally constructed in the 1800s and is available for tours. Plan your visit to the lighthouse while you visit shops, explore the Historical Museum, enjoy the rare wildflowers, and gasp at one of the amazing sunsets, for which the island is famous. The ***Historical Museum*** has exhibits of Indian artifacts, dating back to 200 B.C. It also maintains extensive exhibits, devoted to the Finnish colony, that thrived during the homesteading and lumbering era. In addition, there are geological oddities, historical maps, photos of early settlers, cemetery lists, and more.

Day - 2 – Unique Places – This island has natural wonders that are found in few other places if anywhere. Rock hounds and collectors, will want to take the time to visit the ***Fossil Ledges***. You will need specific directions to get to the ledges. They are north and east of the Four Corners, in the same general direction as the Maxton Plains. From the Interpretive Signs for the Maxton Plains, to the Ledges, involves about 45 minutes of travel. After crossing a swamp and traveling an old two track, one reaches the parking area. After that, all that is left, is a very short hike to the shoreline.

The shoreline at the ledges, is easily walk-able for about a mile. There is a large limestone outcropping near the trail, where there are several orange saltwater fossils. Picking up the broken stones along the shoreline, will reveal all kinds plant and animal fossils, all saltwater species. The lake is beautiful here but remember that it drops off to a depth of more than 6o feet. Many varieties of wildlife can be found on the drive to the ledges and back. Some folks have even reported spotting a bear or two.

Another very rare natural feature on Drummond Island, is an area called the ***Maxton Plains***. This flatland area is a unique grassland, called an alvar. Alvars are extremely rare plant communities, existing on limestone bedrock. Alvars are only found in parts of Canada, the United States, and Sweden. These plains are grasslands, growing on very thin soil, consisting of bulrush sedge and ragwort, prairie dropseed, prairie smoke, and Indian paintbrush. There are even fields of Prairie Smoke, sprouting up through the cracks in the rocks. The Maxton Plains on Drummond Island, at about 2 miles by 4 miles, is one of the largest alvars remaining in North America.

There are several islands out in the bay. If you boat out to Cedar Island, there is a ***Blue Heron Heronry,*** high in the trees on the north side. Here the Blue Herons gather to breed in the spring and early summer. This is quite a distance from the mainland, so keep alert for changing weather conditions.

Day - 3 - Nature Day - Rainbow Trail - Harbor Island - Bird Watching

Getting to the natural wonders, on and around the island, can be accomplished on a hike, skiing, a kayak or canoe, and even sailing. Here are three favorites from among the variety of nature areas to enjoy. A short distance from the intersection of Maxton Cross Road and Maxton Road, is the trailhead for the ***Rainbow Trail***. The trail is about five miles long, with a number of loops, that afford shorter hikes. It goes through stands of trees over mostly even or gently rolling ground. That makes it excellent for cross country skiing in the winter. The most unusual feature of this trail is the frequency of rainbows seen there, hence the name.

The ***Harbor Island National Wildlife Refuge*** is northwest of Drummond Island, in Potagannissing Bay. This island truly is a pristine wilderness, as it has never been timbered or dredged. At nearly 700 acres in size, there are several distinct ecosystems, and there are old-growth stands of trees to admire. There is a large marsh that runs around the main harbor, and on the east side across from Bald Island, there is a rare stand of mature White Pines. Harbor Island is open for day use only, no fires and no camping.

No matter how you get around the island, this is a ***bird watchers*** paradise. The forests and shorelines are home to several species of woodpeckers, the ruby-throated hummingbird, lots of finch species, sparrows, blackbirds, crows, ravens, owls, hawks, osprey, and eagles, as well as several kinds of water birds. With more than a dozen distinct ecosystems, this list is just the beginning of the bird species that visit the island or make it their home. Expect to find raptors, herons, flickers, warblers, thrushes, vireos singing their beautiful songs, and flycatchers.

Winter Fun – If you snowmobile, you can come directly out to the island, to explore the miles of trails. Cross country skiing and snow shoe hiking are favorite activities on the trails that crisscross the island. For those arriving by car or snowmobile, a 32-vehicle car ferry, the Drummond Islander IV, operates throughout the winter months via a channel that is kept open.

Along The Way – Two other special activities are available. There are more than a dozen shipwrecks to explore, including the *"Mystery Shipwreck"*. There is a vessel sitting nearly upright, in 50 feet of water. It appears to be a barge and is more than 60 feet long. The identity and history of the wreck are not known. With all of this natural splendor, Drummond Island has become a favorite destination for a Fall Color Getaway. The unique habitat and ecosystems produce such fantastic color, that the island has an annual *Fall Color Festival*.

Getting There - The ferry departs at least once every hour, year round.

Back Roads Lodging – Choices range from cabins and B&B's, to Golf Resorts. Visit the Tourism Association visitors center or website to check availability.

www.drummondislandchamber.com – 906-493-5245

AL CAPONE

ONCE

OWNED

A

HOUSE

IN

FRANKFORT

Frankfort Getaway

Frankfort is a beautiful town on Lake Michigan. Regardless of which route you take to get there, you will be treated to a gorgeous panorama as you crest the hill. Spread out below is the Betsie River Valley with the picturesque town of Frankfort framed by forested hills, golden beaches, and the great ships out on Lake Michigan. Downtown looks out over Betsie Bay, which stretches for nearly a mile, from the mouth of the river to Lake Michigan. Much of the waterfront is dedicated to green space and parks. Getting around the area is easy due to the excellent system of walking and biking trails that are an integral part of the community.

Day 1 – Around Town - Downtown Frankfort is as cool as a downtown can be. There are several excellent locally owned and most of the services needed on a getaway. You can find gifts, art, apparel and even a real live independent book store. There are a range of dining options from a really good bakery to fusion cuisine. One dining spot that has been a favorite for years is the restaurant inside the *Hotel Frankfort*, located just a few blocks from the beach. Exploring Frankfort by bicycle is made easier by the existence of the *Beach To Beach Trail*, one of the nicest urban trails in Michigan. From Mineral Springs Park, the trail heads east along the shoreline of Betsie Bay with a short bend around the city docks, and then south along the lake again. It is not unusual to hear the beautiful song of the Warbling Vireo along this trail.

All manner of waterfowl will be on the bay, including swans most times of the year. If you cross M-22 at the southern end of the trail past the bay, you can ascend the Audubon platform for a panoramic view of the extensive marshes along the Betsie River.

Some people travel to Frankfort on another trail, the *Betsie Valley Trail*. Very scenic, the Betsie Valley Trail is 22 miles long and extends from Frankfort through Elberta and Beulah to Thompsonville. From Frankfort to Beulah it is non-motorized. All of it is excellent for bicycles and pedestrian use. The 6 miles from Frankfort to Mollineaux Rd. is asphalt and is good for roller-blading.

Day 2 – Scenic Drives - Frankfort is perfect as a base for touring the surrounding area. M- 22 is the road that runs north and south along Lake Michigan. One day trip is heading north to Empire and the *Sleeping Bear Dunes*. The dunes area is famous, but one spot that shouldn't be missed is the *Pierce Stocking Scenic Drive*. The drive loops through over 7 miles of forest and sand dunes. There are world-class views of the Glen Lakes, Sleeping Bear Dunes, and Lake Michigan. At one spot you are hundreds of feet above the lake shore, a perfect place to watch the sun set. By the way, there is a hidden beach just north of Frankfort. Head north on M-22 to Esch Rd. and go west. That road will reach Otter Creek and one of the best beaches in the Sleeping Bear Dunes.

Traveling south out of Frankfort on M-22 provides for another series of beautiful vistas. After crossing the bridge, the land begins to rise. As you climb on the winding road you will come to a couple of scenic view turn offs, they are really worth it. From one of these spots, the entire *Betsie River Valley* is spread out below. The scene includes the Frankfort lighthouse and a vast expanse of Lake Michigan. Further south is the Arcadia pull off. Everybody stops for the incredible view from hundreds of feet above the lake.

Between the overlooks are a number of side roads. The *Gravity Mystery* can be found at the junction of Joyfield and Putney roads. On that corner you will see an old church that is more than 100 years old. Turn south at the church onto Putney Road. Drive downhill about fifty yards past the church. There will be pine trees just ahead on your right. Stop your car, keep your foot firmly on the brake, and shift the car into neutral. Be prepared for a surprise. When you take your foot off the brake, your car will immediately start going backwards up the hill, and it will be going quickly enough to startled you, so be ready. You can go down to the curve, turn around and try it going forward. The effect is quite remarkable. Your car will start moving uphill almost immediately and will move much faster than you would think. Call it an optical illusion or haywire gravity, the effect is real and it's lots of fun.

Day 3 – A Bit Of History - The Frankfort - Elberta area brings to mind the fabulous shipping and lumbering heritage that shaped Northern Michigan. As is often the case in our state, the founding of Frankfort was tied to a Great Lakes storm and a fortunate accident. Captain Snow, on a trip out of Buffalo, was caught in a storm that threatened to destroy his ship. The area was wild and unsettled and the Captain was lucky to find the entrance to the Aux Bec Scies River and clear the sandbar. Then next day he found himself in what is now Betsie Bay.

The *Benzie Historical Museum* is housed in an 1887 church building. The museum has exhibits of artifacts pertaining to Benzie County's history, including exhibits on Bruce Catton, a native of Michigan and Pulitzer Prize winner, Carferries, Logging/Agriculture, Railroads, Gwen Frostic and more. The museum also maintains the 1891 Drake School building in Honor, Michigan.

The oldest standing structure in Benzie County, the *Point Betsie Lighthouse*, was built in 1858. The lighthouse stands adjacent to a public beach, consequently, it is easy to get to and has become one of the most photographed lighthouses in America. The lighthouse is positioned at the southern end of the Manitou Passage and remains in use as a navigational aid. Betsie Point and the Betsie River were named the Sawbill or Merganser by the Indians. The lighthouse was built in 1857-58. The light first shone on October 20, 1858 and has been in continuous service for more than 150 years. The structure sits 52 feet above the lake and has a range of about 15 miles. The original lens, and its 1891 replacement, were of the fourth-order Fresnel design. The current light system features a modern acrylic lens from New Zealand.   The lighthouse is open for tours on weekends from Memorial Day to Columbus Day.

Along The Way - This whole region has a reputation for great food and drink. There are a few places that shouldn't be missed. The ***Cabbage Shed*** is in Elberta, directly across the bay. They know how to build a Guinness and they have the best borscht I have ever tasted. One of the most popular nearby destinations is ***St. Ambrose Cellars***, a meadery. Mead is an ancient beverage made from water and fermented honey. The folks at Ambrose make some of the best. They are also beekeepers so have access to several different varieties of honey. Further south in Thompsonville is the Iron Fish Distillery. They are the only distillery in Michigan that is located on a working farm. They produce craft spirits and have already received international recognition. The Iron Fish is a remarkable achievement by a couple of farmers, on a dirt road, working away with their stills. Something is going on there every weekend.

Lodging - ***The Hotel Frankfort*** is a boutique hotel with 17 rooms, some of the best food in the area and is famous for being haunted. The hotel is at 231 Main St. Frankfort, MI 49635 - Phone: (231) 352-8090.

THE

PAULDING

GHOST

LIGHT

APPEARS

TO

FLOAT

ABOVE

THE

FOREST

Ghost Light Getaway

The Ottawa National Forest covers thousands of square miles across Ontonagon County, in the Upper Peninsula of Michigan. These vast forests are threaded by rivers and streams, many of which produce spectacular waterfalls. People have been here since prehistoric days, mining the wealth hidden in the mountains. Since men first began to explore this wild region, there have been legends and mysteries. Fantastic wealth has been discovered, and some unexplained phenomena, as well. One of the most famous of these mysteries is the "Paulding Mystery Light", also known as the *"Ghost Light"*, or the "Paulding Light". It has been featured in Ripley's Believe It or Not, Fact or Fiction, and numerous articles and publications.

The "Paulding Mystery Light", or "Ghost Light", has been a subject of wonder and speculation, for several generations. The "ghost light" appears after dark, in and above the wilderness, surrounding Paulding. Reports of the mysterious light began soon after the area began to be explored, during the logging and mining eras. People reported seeing the light in all seasons and from different areas. These days, it is usually reported from the dead end, on Robbins Road. The locals say the light isn't visible every night, that it appears in different colors, and moving in a variety of directions; sometimes in a straight line and sometimes appearing to bounce around the distant hilltops. At other times, it seems to drop down into the forest itself. If you are going after the "ghost light", it is fun to tour the area by day, and hunt the light by night.

Day 1 - Local Attractions - Adventure Mine - Old Victoria - Rockland Museum

The ***Adventure Mine Tour*** is about 20 minutes away. This is an authentic mine experience. You can choose from a number of tours, all of which, involve a trek underground, with hardhat and light. This destination also has an underground bicycle trail, that is open for special events. ***Old Victoria***, about 25 minutes away, is a restoration of an old mining camp. Log cabins, the company store, and much more, offer a fascinating glimpse of life during the iron mining days. The ***Rockland Historical Museum*** is on the way to Old Victoria. Inside are some rare items from the development of the area. They have an actual section of the Douglas fir pipeline, used at the Victoria Dam. Waters was diverted to the Taylor air compressor to produce energy for the Victoria Mining Company. For over 40 years, the waters of the south and west branches of the Ontonagon River flowed through this cylinder of wood, powering the mine.

Day 2 - Waterfalls Day - Bond Falls - Kakabika Falls - O Kun De Kun Falls – Canyon Falls

World famous ***Bond Falls*** is about a 15 minute drive

from Paulding, and is spectacular in all seasons. The Bond Falls area is very photogenic and a good spot for a picnic. Little known ***Kakabika Falls***, also about 15 minutes away, is reached after a beautiful drive through the forest. You can park just off the road, and view the upper falls from the bridge. There is an unimproved trail along the waterway, which leads to the lower falls. During the spring thaw, or just after a heavy rain, this turns into a roaring cataract that is thrilling because you can stand right next to it. ***O Kun De Kun Falls***, is a bit further, the drive is about 20 minutes. To reach the falls, you have a hike down a fine nature trail of a couple of miles, it is worth it. There are two separate waterfalls. You can walk behind the water at the second waterfall. ***Canyon Falls*** rivals all them. There are a series of falls roaring through a narrow canyon.

Day 3 - Scenic Drive & Day Trip - Lake of the Clouds
The Porcupine Mountains are about 45 minutes away and can easily become a full day. Getting there involves a drive along the shore of Lake Superior. Several sections of the rock strewn shore are excellent for hunting agates. On Route 64, just a few miles from the mountains, is the easily accessible Bonanza Falls. Inside the Porcupine Mountains Park, lies the beautiful ***Lake of the Clouds.*** The scenery from the Lake of the Clouds, during fall color time, is some of the most beautiful in the world. About halfway to the Lake of the Clouds is a bat cave. You can't enter the cave, but there is a small park across the road. It is good spot to watch the bats flying out of

the cave at dusk.

Along The Way - An alternative scenic drive, would be *Lake Gogebic*. The lake is just 30 minutes away, and the road goes all the way around. Lake Gogebic is the largest inland lake in the upper peninsula and is a great fishing destination. Once famous as perhaps the best black bass lake in the world, it remains a destination for gorgeous scenery. Don't be surprised if you spot a black bear along the way.

Back Roads Lodging - The *Running Bear Resort* is a wonderful collection of spacious cabins for an old time getaway "up north", and they are open in winter.

www.runningbearresort.com – 906-827-3208

Heart of the "Thumb" Getaway

The "thumb" of Michigan covers several counties, and is so often over-looked as a getaway destination, that some of the residents refer to it as the "forgotten" digit. It seems odd that this unique region is not on more "to do" lists. While it lacks the roaring waterfalls of the western upper peninsula, and the frenzied shopping districts on Lake Michigan, it is perfect for some relaxation and easy going exploration. There are miles of shoreline, rivers, and streams. There is an extensive network of very excellent trails made from old railroads.

Caro, in the central part of the "thumb", is ideally located for exploring the central counties, while still offering quick access to the museums and lighthouses along the Lake Huron coast. History buffs won't be able to see everything in a week let alone three days, especially if it is historic architecture that you're after. Of course, it isn't all slow paced. There are cool shopping destinations, vineyards, wineries, and fun festivals all around. It will certainly require more than three days to see all the "thumb" has to offer, but here are some ideas to get you started.

Day 1 - Octagon Barn - Sanilac Petroglyphs - These are two of the most unique destinations in the entire state of Michigan. Both are simply one of a kind.
The Octagon Barn, located in Tuscola County, is a short drive east from Caro. Approximately 1 mile east of the

Village of Gagetown, along the Bay City Forestville Road, the barn is a mile north on Richie Road, just south of the Huron County border. This is easily the most unusual barn anywhere in the region. It is the largest timber frame octagon barn in the country at 102 feet across and 70 feet high. When construction began in 1924, it was known as an air castle because the entire vast interior is open and the roof seems to hang above you, suspended in the air. There is a cool harvest festival here each autumn.

The *Sanilac Petroglyphs* are the only verified sandstone glyph carvings in Michigan. Enigmatic, sometimes bizarre, images are carved into a large outcropping of sandstone, out in the forest in Sanilac County. The discovery of these unique carvings was the result of horrendous firestorms, that swept through the "thumb" region, at the end of the lumbering era. Some of the firestorms were so intense that railroad rails were twisted, and entire towns were obliterated. When the strong west winds blew through after one particularly intense forest fire, the topsoil was blown away revealing the long hidden carvings. Many of the more unusual images, like the 6 finger hand and the man with the conical hat, still offer puzzles to be solved. The site is open to the public, best viewed in the summertime. There is a pleasant interpretive walking path on the site that will lead you to a White Pine that survived the fires back in the last century.

Take the Minden Road to Germania Rd. Go south about

1/2 mile and you will reach the park where these remarkable carvings are located.

Day 2 - Road Trip - Take a drive around the tip of the "thumb" to a variety of attractions. Head out to the northeast toward **Port Hope,** on the Lake Huron shore. This is the first of a number of lighthouses and museums on this drive. The route will also take you through the Wind Farm, encompassing miles of huge wind turbines. Route 25 hugs the shoreline and will take you around the tip of the "thumb". Near the tip is the historic town of **Grindstone City.** Here grindstones and millstones were manufactured in the thousands. Many are still scattered around town. A stop at the Grindstone General Store is rewarded by huge ice cream cones. Going across the tip you find the Point Aux Barques Lighthouse. This is also the place to head out into the lake if you want to visit **Turnip Rock.**

Further west is Caseville, and just a bit further is Bayport, on the shore of Saginaw Bay. The Bayport Fish Company brings in a fresh catch every day and also offers smoked fish for sale. There is excellent dining up near the tip, including The Farm, for "heartland" cuisine.

Day 3 - Southern Links Trailway - While there are plenty of water trails, and bicycle routes in the region, the Southern Links Trailway has a lot to offer for hikers, bikers and snow shoers of all skill levels. This rail-trail runs 10 miles, through the communities of Columbiaville,

Otter Lake and Millington, just south of Caro. The trail is paved with smooth asphalt. An adjacent path is offered for equestrian users. A variety of deciduous trees line the trail, and the colors are spectacular in the fall months. Trail users will pass through a mixed rural landscape, including fields, wetlands, forests, and farmland. Local wildlife is plentiful including rabbits, chipmunks, woodchucks, frogs, and turtles. Encounters between the animals and trail users are not uncommon.

Winter Fun – The nearby trails and parks are great for cross country skiing and snowshoe hiking. If you plan your trip for the right time of year, Caseville is well known for a fantastic winter festival.

Along The Way –In Watrousville, the ***Leonard-McGlone House***, built in 1858 by Patrick McGlone, is an example of Greek Revival Architecture. Restoration is planned, since this is an unusual style for a rural area. On the edge of Caro, you can find the Roadhouse Museum. The museum hosts special displays several times a year, it may have been Caro's first store, post-office, and hotel. William Eber Sherman it appears built the Roadhhouse in 1859 from a log cabin. There is a story that it may also have served as a bawdy house, during more colorful times.

Back Roads Lodging - The *Garden Gate B & B* is famous for their gourmet hot chocolate, home-made cakes and cookies, luxurious thick down comforters that lead to sleeping in till mid-morning and a world class collection of *Bing & Grøndahl Christmas Plates*.

In 1895, *Bing & Grøndahl,* created the first in their series of Christmas plates. Designed with a traditional winter scene, in cobalt blue and white, the plates have been released annually for more than 100 years. The under glaze painting technique, allowed for beautiful paintings, which soon made these Danish plates world famous. The color blue was used on the plates, as it was the only color that could withstand the extreme temperatures required, to make this type of under glaze porcelain. The blue and white plates have become symbols of Danish craftsmanship. The collection at the *Garden Gate* includes plates from 1896 to present.

www.gardengatecaro.com – 989-673-2696

HORTON'S

CREEK

IS

A

TROUT

STREAM

ONCE

FREQUENTED

BY

ERNEST

HEMINGWAY

Horton's Creek Getaway

Horton's Creek flows under the Charlevoix/Boyne City Road, approximately one-half mile west of the village of Horton Bay. This small waterway became a famous destination, because Ernest Hemingway fished for trout here, and wrote about the area in his story "Up In Michigan". One way to check out Horton's Creek is via the Rufus Teesdale Nature Preserve. The Little Traverse Conservancy maintains the preserve. As you approach the bridge over the creek, watch for a small sign on the right (north) side of the road. From the parking lot is a footpath to the creek.

Day 1 - Local Destinations - Lavender Farm - Horton Bay General Store - Greensky Hill
Among the myriad attractions in this area is the largest lavender farm in Michigan. A short drive north, on Horton Bay Road, will get you there. Don't worry about the address, you can't miss it. The *Lavender Farm* is a favorite farm visit for tourists, garden clubs, and families. Visitors can enjoy a tour of the fields, join a class in making lavender wands, walk the lavender labyrinth, check out the gift shop, or relax under the big walnut tree, and just enjoy the serene countryside. The farm offers tours and instruction on growing lavender or beekeeping. In the tiny village of Horton Bay, there are a couple of cool shops that are usually only open in the summer months. The *Horton Bay General Store* building has been here since it was built in 1876 and has always been

the center of business and social life in the village. Hemingway frequented the store as a boy and a young man. He described it in the story "Up In Michigan". Just a few miles west of Horton's Creek, is a small sign announcing *Greensky Hill*. This is the site of the all-Indian Pine River Mission, established in the 1830s. The site is now known as Greensky Hill in honor of Peter Greensky, a Chippewa, who preached the gospel and converted native Americans, in the Leelanau, area to Christianity. The church building is still there, and a large Indian cemetery is carefully maintained. There is a rare council site just off the chapel grounds. As you leave the area the drive takes a sharp turn. If you look to the north, from that curve, you will see a half-dozen huge old maple trees. These trees are in a circle and have been bent and twisted. This was a sacred "council", or meeting, site for native American tribes. The trees are on private property but can be clearly seen. Note that this road to Greensky Hill is gravel.

Day 2 – Around Lake Charlevoix - Boyne City Gift Shops - On The Beach Inverted Forest - Cafe Sante - Ironton Ferry

Lake Charlevoix dominates this area. The cool clear waters attract visitors from all over the world. The south side of the lake can be toured easily on a winding road. From Horton's Creek drive into Boyne City. Any time of day, you can get a sumptuous meal at *Cafe Sante'*, don't miss it. Boyne City is usually bustling with activity and is considered one of the best shopping destinations in this whole area. Along the south side of Lake Charlevoix are excellent parks and public beaches. From the beach, if you look across the lake you can locate the *"Inverted Forest"*. There are hundreds of fallen trees on the north side of the lake. Locals, campers, and tourists have taken these fallen trees and stuck them into the sandy bottom of the shallows. So many have been "planted" up-side-down that they now form an "inverted" forest.

Another unique attraction is the *Ironton Ferry*. This car ferry crosses the narrow neck, of the south arm, of Lake Charlevoix. It is a cable ferry and only holds four cars at a time. The whole ride lasts about 5 minutes and is just plain fun. The old signs that listed prices for transporting sheep and cattle are still in place.

Day 3 – Scenic Drive - Ride The Breezeway - Mushroom Houses - Red Mesa Grille

The *"Breezeway"* is a scenic drive that will take you through beautiful hills and quaint towns. It runs from Atwood, near Grand Traverse Bay, through the hills and drumlins to Boyne Falls. The whole drive is about 25 miles and touches the south branch of Lake Charlevoix, where swans are common. The drive runs east and west. As you travel you will go up and down lots of hills. Some of these are drumlins, rare glacial formations. Drumlins are high ridges, formed by the receding glaciers, that run north and south. The "Breezeway", County Road

C-48, is popular with bikers. There are shops, galleries, crafters, and farmers markets along the way.

To get to Atwood, from Horton Bay, takes one through Charlevoix. There are excellent art galleries and some very unusual shops downtown. The real hidden treasures in Charlevoix, are the famous *"mushroom" houses,* created by Earl Young. These unique structures have been called ***Hobbitland***, mushroom homes, elf space, and gnome houses, and the only place you can see them is Charlevoix. The historical society has a tour map of the triangular block, bounded by Park Avenue, Grant Street, and Clinton Street, where many of the houses are.

The eastern end of the Breezeway is in Boyne Falls. It is a short drive back to Horton Bay, through Boyne City, where we make it a point to stop at the ***Red Mesa Grill,*** for exceptional Latin American food.

Along The Way – This area has one of the best ***Morel Mushroom Festivals*** in all of Michigan. On Saturday mornings, in the summer months, the farmers market on the waterfront in Boyne City may be the best in the North

Dunmaglas - The Boyne City Road hugs the north shore of Lake Charlevoix. Between Charlevoix and Horton Bay, is where you will find the Dunmaglas Golf Club. The entrance is a simple parking lot next to an unassuming pro shop. Hidden in the hills and woodlands beyond the practice green, is a golf course that should be on every players list. Ranked as one of the Best 50 Upscale Courses in the United States by Golf Digest, this 6,897-yard masterpiece, features 18 of the most scenic and breathtaking holes you will ever play. They describe this course as golf in its purest form, and they may be right. Every single hole on this golf course is a work of art. Teeing it up on number one, the player will know immediately, that a great round of golf is coming up. A beautiful stream meanders along the left side of the fairway. The green is reached around a gentle dogleg. As on nearly every hole on this course, the player can only see the hole being played.

In addition to the natural beauty on each hole, there are some spectacular views of the hills, and Lake Charlevoix, in the distance. The scenery along numbers 4, 5, and 6 is unrivaled, and the view from the 14th tee, must rank in the top 4 or 5 anywhere in Michigan.

HOUGHTON

LAKE

IS

THE

LARGEST

OF

THE

"OTHER"

GREAT

LAKES

Houghton Lake Getaway

Houghton Lake is Michigan's largest inland lake. Combined with neighboring Higgins Lake, the area has become known as Michigan's, other Great Lakes. The ***Springbrook Inn,*** with its gorgeous rooms, excellent restaurant, and Frog Tiki Bar, is in the center of it all. This area has been a traditional vacation destination, for several generations of Michiganders. While the lakes are the most prominent feature in the region, there is a lot more to do, when you have had enough of the beach. From the Springbrook Inn, in Prudenville, you are minutes from those beaches, boat launches, shopping, dining, hiking, canoeing, and golf courses. There is horseback riding, bird-watching, live theatre, historic destinations, snowmobile trails, cross-country skiing, ice fishing, and seemingly endless nature areas to explore.

Day 1 - Scenic Drives - Around The Lakes - Old 27 Marshlands - Quilt Block Trail - Natural Beauty Road Site seeing around the lake is a relaxing drive, and a good way to get an idea of what this area has to offer. It is a short drive, from ***Houghton Lake to Higgins Lake,*** where one often finds the windsurfers having fun. The roads are in good condition and the routes are well marked. However, from one end of Houghton Lake to the other is more than 40 miles. Most of the shops, theaters and museums are found on this main route. The Old Highway 27, runs north and south, just west of the lakes. The ***Houghton Lake Flats*** is a wildlife restoration project, designed to provide habitat for waterfowl and other wetland species. An observation deck, and handicapped accessible gazebo, provide visitors a place to stop and enjoy the wide variety of birds that now populate the flats. Just a mile further north one can stop and observe Great Blue Herons at a rookery.

The *Roscommon County Quilt Trail,* is a fun and interesting way, to explore this beautiful part of Michigan. Families in this area, have preserved and handed down, traditional family quilts through generations. Now these patterns are displayed on buildings and barns throughout the County. Many of the quilt patterns tell stories about family history and cultures. Use caution when slowing down or stopping to view the quilt blocks, and show respect to the private property, where some of them are located.

About 10 miles north of Prudenville is Lansing Road. The gravel section, between M-18 and County Road 100, has been designated a *Natural Beauty Road*. The road runs through a stand of White Birch trees believed to be the largest tract left in lower Michigan.

Day 2 - Nature Areas - Kirtland's Warbler - Ogemaw Nature Park - Lost Twin Lakes Pathway

Kirtland's Warbler Viewing – In the northern part of Roscommon County, is an area with sandy soils and small grassy openings, scattered throughout the forest of young jack pine trees. These conditions are the unique habitat, that is required for the endangered Kirtland's Warbler to nest and breed. There are only about a few thousand of these birds left, and they return to Jack Pines of Roscommon County, every year.

Ogemaw Nature Park – On West Rose City Road is the Ogemaw Nature Park. This is a cool place to take the kids. Older deer that have been rescued are in the park and visitors can feed them. There are also fawns, goats, and a pig or two. The park has a picnic area and has food available to feed to the animals. The park is usually open from noon to 7:00 p.m.

The *Lost Twin Lakes Pathway,* has features that few other local trails can match. This trail has remained relatively unknown due to its remote location off a gravel road and, that for many years, it was just plain too wet and soggy for casual hikers. The trail is in part of the Au Sable State Forest. The loop runs a bit over 3 miles and became an Eagle Scout project a few years ago. They built a number of bridges and boardwalks over the wettest parts of the trail. If you are looking for a pleasant walk in the woods, this is the pathway for you. There are century-old white pines that survived the lumbering days. Some of these pines are as much as five feet around. In addition, there are ridges, sinkholes, wetlands, and swamps along with those small lakes, from which the pathway gets its name. Lost Twin Lakes is open to Nordic skiing, snowshoeing and mountain biking.

Day 3 - Historic Attractions - Fireman's Memorial - Historical Village - CCC (Civilian Conservation Corps) Museum

At the *Fireman's Memorial,* a bronze firefighter standing twelve feet tall and weighing around 2,000 pounds, is the centerpiece of the site. The statue was created by Michigan craftsman Edward Chesney. The grounds include picnic and play areas. If you visit this memorial on a weekday, like I did, you may find that you are the only person there. Wandering the grounds, and studying the names of the fallen, is an emotional experience. This memorial is dedicated to the members of that unselfish organization of men and women, who hold devotion to duty above personal risk, who count sincerity of service above personal comfort and convenience, and who strive unceasingly to find better ways of protecting the lives, homes, and property of their fellow citizens, from the ravages of fire and other disasters.

Each year, usually during the 3rd week of September, a festival is held in remembrance of these brave citizens. During this festival there is a parade, antique equipment demonstration, a memorial service, a light parade, music, dancing, and emergency crew competitions. The Firemen's Memorial is just south of Roscommon about 1/2 mile east of M-18.

The *Historical Village,* on the south end of Houghton Lake, is one of the most extensive in Michigan. There are 11 restored buildings from the 1800s to visit on the self-guided tour, including a schoolroom, Blue Star Museum, town hall, dress shop, general store, doctor's office/ pharmacy, barber shop, a homestead, a chapel and others. The schoolhouse is an original hand-hewn log structure, built in 1876 to serve the children of Edna, now named Prudenville.

The *Village Days* festival brings the village to life, through demonstrations, and guides in period costumes. All of the buildings are open for the event, and are operating just as they would have, when originally built. The event also includes craft and musical demonstrations. During the Great Depression of the 1930's, access to social welfare programs required elbow grease. Michigan, and the rest of the nation, had to roll up their sleeves and work their way out of trouble. The *Civilian Conservation Corps* was formed to "put Americans back to work". Over 100,000 of Michigan's young men journeyed to CCC Camps all over the state, to work on reforestation and conservation projects. Between 1933 and 1942, these workers planted more than 480 million trees, constructed 7,000 miles of truck trails, 504 bridges, and 222 buildings.

The *CCC (Civilian Conservation Corps) Museum,* exhibits photographs and artifacts to paint the picture of the CCC workers day-to-day life and accomplishments.

The grounds are across from North Higgins Lake State Park, on North Higgins Lake Drive, and include a replica CCC barracks building with exhibits.

Winter Fun – Back in 1951, a couple of the guys were trying to figure out how to pass the long winter months on Houghton Lake. They decided to have a festival out on the ice of the frozen lake. A nationwide contest was held to come up with a name for the event. They eventually settled on *Tip-Up-Town USA*, a reference to the little flag on an ice fishing rig, that signals a bite. Today, the festival is huge, requiring more than 200 volunteers. Events, like sled dogs, polar dip, medallion hunt, and dozens of contests and parades are held over two weekends in January. When you have had enough of the ice, the Frog Tiki Bar is like a trip to the tropics.

Along The Way - North Higgins Lake State Park has programs and guided hikes all summer. The *Anchor Inn* in the "Heights" area is said to be haunted. There are beaches all around the lake with varying amenities.

Back Roads Lodging – *Springbrook Inn* - Locals will tell you that the East Bay Grille inside the Springbrook Inn prepares the best prime rib in the North. Their rooms are large, and each one has a full size hot tub.

www.springbrookinn.com – 989-366-6347

Iron County Getaway

Iron County, Michigan is known as the ***Bald Eagle Capital of Michigan,*** with more than a dozen nesting pairs. Folks go to Iron County for the pure air, sparkling waterfalls, and silent forests, gorgeous mountainous country. Special as the natural beauty is, there is much more. Discover the old flooded mines, legendary thieves, a humongous fungus, and rare musical instruments, helping make theatre come alive.

The ***Hardwood Hotel***, with its Bald Eagle Totem Pole, is a perfect headquarters for exploring one of the wildest, most pristine, counties left in Michigan. Access to miles of snowmobile trails is offered from the parking area, for winter sports enthusiasts. It is only a short drive to waterfalls, hiking, and the shops and museums of nearby, Crystal Falls, or the incredible exhibits at the Iron County Historical Museum in Caspian.

Day 1 - Historic Sites - One of the best ways to explore the history of Iron County, is to drive the ***Iron County Heritage Trail*** - 14 distinct sites tell the story of Iron County. These sites are on, or just off, the designated Iron County Heritage Route. Sites along the 36 mile drive include: Iron County Heritage Museum, Pentoga Park Indian Burial Grounds, Alpha Circle Historic District, Iron County Courthouse, Mansfield Disaster Location and Pioneer Church, Amasa Museum, Fortune Pond, Bewabic State Park, Larson Park, Apple Blossom

Trail, Lake Ottawa Recreation Area, Mile Post Zero & Treaty Tree, and Camp Gibbs Recreation Area.

Iron County Historical Museum - Of all the museums I have visited, this is one of the most impressive. You may want to plan for the better part of a day, because this place is full of unusual and extensive exhibits. The main building has the major exhibits, including a diorama consisting of over 100 miniature pieces carved to scale showing a logging camp and work in the woods. The 85' diorama, is believed to be the largest of its kind, in the world. Other fine exhibits include the Wildlife Art Gallery, a replica of a "spirit house", as found in the Indian Burial Ground at Pentoga Park, and there are a number of "stills", and other equipment, that date from Prohibition and the "Rum Rebellion". Outside is the Homestead exhibit of six log buildings, circa 1890-1900, which demonstrate what pioneer life was like.

The Lumber Camp, has four log buildings and equipment. The Mining Area, includes The Landmark mine head structure for hoisting ore, a replica of an underground drift and underground equipment. The Transportation Area, has the 1890 depot and a car barn, housing a 1911 streetcar. There is also an enormous Steam Roller here, marked Case, that is believed to be one of just three in the world. The Victorian Area, includes the Carrie Jacobs Bond House, built in 1890, and an early one room school.

Day 2 - Waterfalls - A trip to the famous Horserace Rapids, will take you to a deep river gorge. From the parking area, a set of stairs has been installed to aid the steep descent to the river. These roaring rapids are considered a challenge for even expert white-water canoeists and kayakers. *Horserace Rapids* is south of Crystal Falls. The road is well maintained, but it is gravel. There are several other very accessible waterfalls including Chicaugon Falls, Duppy Falls, Jumbo Falls, and Long Lake Falls.

Chicaugon Falls – take U.S. 2 to Long Lake Road, north about 3 miles until you see the big brown barn. Take Raymer Drive and watch for the signs.

Duppy Falls and *Jumbo Falls* are in the northwest of the county and can be visited in the same day. *Duppy Falls* – take U.S. 2 west to Forest Highway 16. Go north on FS 16 – about 19 miles to USFS Road 3610 (just north of Tepee Lake). USFS Road 3610 is just a landmark to indicate you are getting close. Continue on Forest Highway16 about 0.7 miles to the first trail road going west (left). Travel 0.2 miles down Forest Service Trail Road 3645 to a grass clearing next to State Creek. There is a trail to the creek and a small wood bridge. The falls can be found by walking a trail southwest. It is about half a mile to the falls.

Jumbo Falls is located just south south-west of Kenton. From Duppy Falls, just travel north on Forest Highway

16, a bit over 5 miles, to Kenton. Turn west (left) on M-28 and travel Golden Glow Road just past the Jumbo River stream crossing. Turn south (left) and travel a mile and a half to Golden Glow Road W. Turn east (left) and travel 1/3 mile to USFS Road 4589-b and turn southeast (right). Just over one mile is a parking area for the falls. A short trail takes you upstream to the falls through old growth conifer trees.

Long Lake Falls is west of Long Lake, on Chicaugon Creek. From Crystal Falls, go west on U.S. 2 for about five miles to Long Lake Road. Go north and travel three miles around the north end of Long Lake to a gravel access road on the west side of Long Lake Road marked by some private camp signs. Turn west and take the fork to the right and then the next intersection straight off the gravel onto a trail road. The intersections, on this last access trail, are marked with homemade "falls" signs leading toward the Long Lake Falls. After a half mile, park out of the way at two signs, "Falls and Horton." It is about a half mile walk down the hill on a trail to the waterfall.

Day 3 - Hiking Trails - The trails of Iron County offer everything from cross country skiing to white water rapids to ancient burial grounds. Here are three of our favorites.

Apple Blossom Trail - The trail starts across the road from the Iron County Historical Museum in Caspian. It is a paved, wheel-chair accessible, trail that winds along the Iron River, and roughly follows the original railroad line. The spot where Harvey Mellon first discovered iron ore is on the trail. There is a view of an abandoned quarry that is now stocked with trout, and a small waterfall on the Iron River. At the trail head is a sign, speaking the "language of dogs".

Lake Mary Plains Pathway - Locally known as the Glidden Lake Foot Paths, there are three different loops starting at the parking area at Glidden Lake. The lake is on Lake Mary Road about five miles east of Crystal Falls and south of Route 69. The trails are from 3 to 4 miles long. They are well maintained and are marked with signs about every half mile.

Pentoga Park - This is known as the Brule River Trail and starts in Pentoga Park. The trail crosses Route 424 and spans about 2.5 miles to the Brule River. Another trail in this park, is a mile long trail, that ends at the Indian Ceremonial Bowl. A unique feature of this park is the Indian Burial Ground, with several "Spirit Houses" preserved on the site.

Along The Way – Humongous Fungus - Crystal Theatre - The Split Rock

Discovered in 1988, the *Humongous Fungus,* is one of the largest and oldest living organisms in the world. While most of it is underground, it still covers almost 40 acres, and weighs in at about 100 tons. It is the species called, Armillaria Bulbosa, and the mushrooms it produces are commonly called button or "honey mushroom." The mushroom is the only edible part of the fungus. Armillaria Bulbosa is very common, occurring in hardwood forests in North America, Europe, and Japan. Although visitors want to see the "Humungous Fungus" for themselves, it is mostly underground, except for tiny offshoots, that poke through the surface in the fall. There isn't really much to see, however, attending the *Humongous Fungus Festival* can make up for that; great fun, edible mushrooms, and you can get the Tee Shirt. The festival is usually in August.

The "*Split Rock*" is located just south of Crystal Falls, as you travel towards the Wisconsin border on US 2 / 141. It is right at the intersection of 424, which turns to Alpha, MI. The rock was split in half by a tree, that managed to grow up right through the rock. Old-timers claim the split rock was an important landmark, for pioneers and explorers, following the old Indian trails. The highway department has placed a sign at the site, the old tree is now dead.

The *Crystal Theatre* is in downtown Crystal Falls. While the exterior looks a lot like other old theaters, this one has some special features inside. It has the distinction of possessing the largest theatre pipe organ, in Michigan's Upper Peninsula. The organ, consisting of 3 manuals (keyboards), and 21 ranks (sets of pipes), was originally built in 1927, by the M.P. Möller Company of Hagerstown, Maryland. There are more than 1,600 pipes, installed in the on-stage chambers, ranging in size from half an inch to over 16 feet in length. In addition, there is a battery of actual tuned percussion, drums, traps and sound effects, installed in two chambers, located on either side of the proscenium. This historic theatre has local school drama plays, instrumentalists, bands, singers, talent shows, and organ concerts, on its impressive Moeller Theater Pipe Organ.

Another long-time destination in Crystal Falls is *"Winks Woods"*. One of the "must visit" gift shops in all of the upper peninsula, they are open all year.

Back Roads Lodging – The Hardwood Hotel is on Route 141 near Amasa. Also known as *Tall Pines*, the Hardwood Hotel is also home to the Pine Cone Cafe and the Tall Pines Grocery.

www.tallpinesamasa.com – 906-822-7713

THE

SHACK

IS

A

TRADITIONAL

LOG

LODGE

ON

ROBINSON

LAKE

Jugville Shack Getaway

This is the getaway, for those who want to "get away from it all", in a quiet and secluded place, yet have shops, attractions, and dining close at hand, just in case. If you are after more than just relaxation, there are unique attractions in this area that you simply will not find in most rural counties. A thorough exploration of the region can fill several days. A scenic back roads drive is part of the getaway. Robinson Lake, and the Shack in Jugville, are just 44 Miles from Muskegon, 65 Miles from Grand Rapids, and 35 Miles from Big Rapids, Michigan.

After a relaxing back roads drive, this spot, on Robinson Lake, offers summer activities which include hiking, swimming, fishing, riding paddle boats, sitting on a covered porch, or just relaxing by the lake. The flower gardens are works of art, and the trails are great for bird watching. You could just stay at the Shack, enjoying the delicious meals they serve. Then have fun on the trails for walking and hiking, paddle boats, gazebos and country porches, reading and relaxing, billiards, ping pong, shuffleboard, exercise room, more relaxing at the fireside, a visit to the on site museum, and banana splits every night. You could just stay, but there are unique attractions nearby.

Day 1 - Nature Day - Loda Wildflower Sanctuary - Coolbough Creek Trails

The ***Loda Wildflower Sanctuary*** is the only wildflower sanctuary in a National Forest. Through more than 70 acres, and a hiking trail of about 1 1/2 miles, you can discover a sampling of wildflowers that used to cover much of lower Michigan. In fact, more than 200 plants have been identified, and you can find them easily by following the trail map brochures provided near the trail head. In addition to the wildflowers, there are birds galore. The wildflower sanctuary has a bird checklist available, listing more than 120 varieties of birds, found in the different habitats.

The Loda Lake Wildflower Sanctuary includes a small spring-fed lake, a wetland area, a creek, and marshy areas. There is an oak forest, pine plantations, and the remains of an old farm site. This is a gorgeous place for a quiet break or a full day. There is a picnic area and there are rustic facilities. There are no shops or services, and it is important to note that, you will have to drive a gravel road to get there. The Loda Wildflower Sanctuary is in northern Newaygo county about 6.5 miles north of White Cloud, off route 37.

Coolbough Creek - Discover 14+ miles of trails containing very diverse habitats. Hikers can make their way through white pine and white oak forests full of song birds, catalog numerous types of butterflies, and wildflowers on the prairie remnants. A section of the trail follows the shores of the wetland, to the cool running waters of Bigelow and Coolbough Creeks.

Day 2 - Shrine of the Pines - A few miles north of White Cloud is the town of Baldwin, Michigan. On the banks of the Pere' Marquette River is a small museum, known as the ***Shrine of the Pines***. Don't be misled by the small size of the building, and the simple exterior. Inside is the largest collection of rustic White Pine furniture in the world. It is all exquisitely beautiful, all the work of one man, Raymond W. Overholzer, and all done by hand, without the aid of power tools. The tour is well worth it and very informative. The Shrine is open in summer only.

While in town it is a good idea to visit ***Jones Ice Cream.*** They are located in downtown Baldwin, you really can't miss it. Those in the know consider this the best ice cream in Michigan, and families return again and again, generation after generation. If you are looking for special Michigan items, check out ***Pandora's Box*** across the street from the ice cream shop.

Day 3 - Croton Hardy Dam - Hardy Dam, a few miles upstream from Newaygo, was built in 1931. It is gigantic, actually the largest hydroelectric plant in the Lower Peninsula, producing enough electricity for a city of 24,000 people. This structure has turned the upstream part of the Muskegon River, into the 4,000+ acre Hardy Dam Pond. The pond has nearly 50 miles of mostly undeveloped shoreline, with no private cottages or homes on it. Downstream is the Hardy Dam Rustic Nature Trail where, at times, it's so quiet in the woods you forget all about the generators, power lines, and spillways just upstream.

Sailors Pines - You can still walk through a stand of near virgin pine trees in the lower peninsula. In the 1920s the lumber era was passing, and Mr. William Sailors was reviewing his timber holdings. He found that he owned a stand that was maturing, but the trees were not yet large enough to harvest. He had participated in the lumber boom and had seen the giant pines toppled forest by forest but decided to preserve this last stand of pines. Today you can wander through them and see what lumberjacks would have seen in the 1800s. Some of these are now giants, 30 inches in diameter and 100 feet tall. This stand of pines is dedicated to Mr. and Mrs. Sailors. The area is managed by their children. The pines are located on 52nd Street, a quarter mile east of Locust Avenue, near the Croton Hardy Dam.

The ***River Stop Cafe,*** in downtown Newaygo, is one of a very few cafes or bistros around Michigan, that are on our must visit list, again and again. The food is delicious, and the menu always has some unusual taste delight to try. The atmosphere is relaxing, soft music is playing, great coffee and WiFi.

Along The Way - *Dark Skies* - Out here in the rural areas, Michigan is blessed with very little light pollution. City dwellers are often amazed at the stars and galaxies, that fill our night skies. To see some spectacular close ups of those stars, you could visit the Stephen F. Wessling Observatory that is only minutes away from *The Shack*. This is a unique environmental center and astronomical observatory, that is open to the public. The Observatory is located on the Kropscott Centennial Farm, on the corner of Baseline and Stone Road, and is widely known as the Kropscott Farm Environmental Center.

The facility has telescopes of various designs and sizes, including: an 18" Obsession reflector, the 12.5" Raymond B. Larson telescope, and a variety of 6" to 8" computerized and non-computerized, reflecting telescopes. All of these are available for the public for star viewing, personally operated, with the assistance of the Newaygo County Dark Sky Astronomers.

Treasure in Mecosta – If you love books and bookstores, a day trip to Mecosta will really pay off. The Book Gallery contains one of the largest collections of used and rare books, in all of northern Michigan. Stacks and stacks of old books in room after room are waiting. The staff knows where everything is. They are usually open on weekends.

Golf - There are 5 different golf courses within 10 miles of the resort.

Winter Fun - Relaxing by the fireplace is my recommendation, but the pristine wilderness and scenic hiking paths are great for cross country skiing and snow shoeing. It is a little wild out there, as there are no groomed trails in Newaygo county. In addition to the trails at The Shack and Coolbough Creek, there are numerous other trails nearby, such as, the famous North Country Trail Network, Loda Lake Wildflower Sanctuary, Hungerford Lake Trail, and Branstrom Park.

Back Roads Lodging - *The Shack*, a traditional log lodge, is nestled in 100 acres of woods on the shore of Robinson Lake, in the small town of Jugville, just a few miles west of White Cloud.

www.theshackbedandbreakfast.com – 231-924-6683

Konteka Getaway

Located in historic White Pine, in the upper peninsula, the ***Konteka Resort***, has every amenity necessary, to provide a comfortable and secure lodging while exploring northwestern Ontonagon County, Michigan. This is one resort that can guarantee you will see ***black bears.*** The Konteka is just a couple of miles from the shore of Lake Superior, and only a 20 minute drive from the Lake of the Clouds, in the heart of the Porcupine Mountains. The shore of Lake Superior is covered with beautiful rocks, that include the coveted agate. There is an old shipwreck, off the mouth of the Mineral River, that isn't difficult to reach. About halfway to the Lake of the Clouds, is a cave with a bat population. At nightfall, the entire colony may come flying out. This is just a sampling of things to do on this getaway.

Activity at the mine that supported ***White Pine*** has dwindled so, there is little left of the town. However, the Konteka still thrives in this vast wilderness, part of the Ottawa National Forest, and there are dozens of things to see and do, within easy driving distance. Lake Gogebic is to the south, iron mine tours to the east, and 4 waterfalls on one road to the west, plus it is just a short drive to the famous Mystery Light in Paulding, to name a few.

Day 1 - Waterfalls - With over 90 waterfalls, big and small in the area, you will have to pick and choose, or mix some in with other destinations. Local favorites include nearby Bonanza Falls, just south of The Konteka on M-74, the more famous Agate Falls and Bond Falls, then the remote, awesome, O Kun De Kun & Kakabika Falls are just waiting to be discovered.

Bonanza Falls is very easy to get to, and there is history behind the beauty. Tales of fabulous silver deposits have been around since the earliest days of exploration in the upper peninsula. Silver mixed, but unalloyed with native copper, known as "free silver", has been brought out of the copper mines. The legends grew large, since most of the silver was smuggled out of the mines, in the miners dinner pails.

One silver deposit did exist, near the Iron River, just inland from Lake Superior. Bonanza Falls was named by Austin Corser, in honor of his discovery of a rich pocket of silver ore in 1855. He kept this discovery secret for seventeen years, because he couldn't file a claim until a government land grant for a proposed railroad expired, in 1872. Once the discovery became public, the "silver rush" was on, including the establishment of the nearby town of Silver City. Early assays came in between $185.00 to $1,716.00 per ton. Unfortunately, the first silver ingot refined from the ore, came out at $33.00 per ton. The upshot was, that it would cost more to mine the silver, than it was worth. By 1876, the "silver rush" was over. Then, the lumber companies arrived. The Greenwood Lumber Company flourished for a while beginning in 1908, and the waterfall became known as Greenwood Falls. A forest fire wiped out most of the buildings in 1921, and now there are no buildings remaining, nature has reclaimed everything. In 1998, this spot was named a heritage site. The gravel parking area for Bonanza Falls, is on M-64, just north of the Konteka. It is just a short walk to the falls.

South and east of White Pine is Paulding, where the famous *Bond Falls* can be found. Well known and frequently visited, it is a beautiful spot that is easy to access. About 10 miles north of Paulding, is Bruce Crossing. A few miles north of the crossing, is the trail to a waterfall, where you can actually walk behind the falling water. Named after an Ojibway chief, *O Kun de Kun Falls,* is one of the largest waterfalls in Ontonagon county. It is not as large as Bond Falls, or Agate Falls, but it is just as scenic, and far wilder. The waterfall is unusual in that it is an actual plunge falls. Only a handful of the many waterfalls around Lake Superior are plunge falls. You can go behind the falls if you want, but you need to be careful and sure footed.

O Kun De Kun falls is found at the end of a nature hike. The sign says it is 1.3 miles to the falls. There are actually two trails. One is wide and fairly smooth. The other is more of a trail, wet and rough almost like a wild animal trail, with lots of ups and downs. If you take the wide smooth trail, it is easy going and you will come to a suspension bridge, that is part of the North Country Trail.

However, you will miss the first waterfall found on the narrow trail, which I think, is better than the main falls. The trail head to the falls is located on the east side of US 45, about 8 miles north of Bruce Crossing. There are signs for the small parking area.

Day 2 - Scenic Drives - Black River Harbor - Lake Gogebic - Color Tours

Less than an hour from the Konteka, just across the county line is the Black River. Highway, Route 513. This is the Black River National Scenic Byway, running 15 miles from U.S. 2 north through the Ottawa National Forest, to the Black River Harbor. The Black River Harbor is on Lake Superior and is one of only two harbors in the National Forest System. The section of the Black River that flows here is enclosed by pines, hardwoods, and hemlocks.

The road follows the course of the river as it drops from the highlands down to Lake Superior. As you drive along, you can pull off into parking areas to view and photograph the waterfalls. Waterfalls in the order you encounter them are, *Conglomerate Falls*, *Potawotami* & *Gorge Falls*, *Sandstone Falls* and *Rainbow Falls*.

All of the falls are accessible in the warm seasons. Though they are all on the same river, each waterfall is different from the others. Potawotami Falls is the easiest to reach and has a barrier-free access trail, leading from the parking lot for Gorge Falls. The other falls can be reached by trails that vary from easy to downright tricky. In some cases, there are steep stairs to climb. ***Rainbow Falls*** is spectacular, throwing enough mist into the air during its plunge, to produce the rainbows that give it its name. At the Black River Harbor, there is plenty of parking, a spacious picnic area, and a foot bridge across the river to the shoreline.

As you make your way along the Black River Road, you will see a gigantic structure jutting into the sky. That is the world's largest ski jump up, on Copper Peak. In the summer and fall, visitors can take the chairlift up, and then an elevator to the top, about 240 feet above the crest of the hill. In ideal weather conditions, you can see 100 miles across Lake Superior, to the Minnesota, Canadian Border.

Another scenic drive is just 10 miles south of White Pine, on Route 64. It begins at the northern end of ***Lake Gogebic***, the largest inland lake in the upper peninsula. Lake Gogebic has 36 miles of shoreline, with the added beauty of being within the Ottawa National Forest. Lake Gogebic itself is in two counties, and in two time zones. The north half of the lake is in Ontonagon County, and the Eastern Time zone. The south half of the lake is in Gogebic County, and the Central Time zone.

Black River and Lake Gogebic make good ***color tours***. Often overlooked, but never forgotten, is a short c***olor*** *tour* from Ontonagon, through Rockland, and then either to Victoria or down 26 toward Greenland. This short drive, under 50 miles round trip, is spectacular any time of year.

Day 3 - Unique Destinations - Ontonagon Lighthouse - Old Victoria - Adventure Mine Tour - Lake of the Clouds - The Bat Cave

The ***Ontonagon Lighthouse*** has been fully restored and is operated by the Ontonagon County Historical Society. The lighthouse is open six days a week. Tours begin at the Museum complex downtown, then move out to the lighthouse complex, and culminate in the lantern room, at the top of the lighthouse. From that spot visitors have a great view of the lake, harbor, and the unique profile of the Porcupine Mountains 20 miles distant. The stories and details, that are included in the tour, make it a real treat. One story is about the discovery that a lantern, suspended from the steeple of a Church located high atop a hill at the town of Rockland 12 miles inland, could be seen from a great distance out on Lake Superior. By lining up the Church light with the Ontonagon Lighthouse, ships could steer straight into the Harbor at night! In October 1975, the Ontonagon Lighthouse was placed on the National Register of Historic Places.

While touring the lighthouse and museum, visitors are introduced to the mining industry that played such an important role, in the history of this beautiful area. There are a number of mines in the area that offer tours. For a variety of tours, and an authentic experience, the *Adventure Mine* is a great choice. The Adventure Mine operated from 1850 to 1920 and is one of the best preserved mine sites of its age. Like almost all of the mining locations of Copper Country, the Adventure was opened on existing, prehistoric excavations located on Adventure Bluff. These prehistoric workings date to about 5,000 years before the present-day, and were very extensive. Although the Adventure always showed great promise, and millions of dollars were spent pursuing that dream, the mine always won out in the end. It never produced a profit.

During the tour, you can experience the mine as the miners did, over 160 years ago, with a single light on your hard hat. There are no other lights underground - just like it was for them. Want to go where no one has been in 100+ years? The Captain's Tour, on the 2nd level, had been flooded since the mine closed in 1920, except for a brief two week period in the 1980s, when prospectors were mining some of the stopes for copper specimens. Now open, they have discovered that there are many artifacts left in place, including the rails from the tram system, timbers from loading chutes, shovels, powder boxes, a few tram cars, and even an old pump, used for the original dewatering of the mine. The Adventure Mining Company is only a 30 minute drive from the Konteka.

Several hundred acres of old growth forest surround one of the most popular, must see attractions in the Porcupine Mountains, the *Lake of the Clouds*. A short hike from the parking area will take you to spots where you can enjoy the spectacular view. At any time of year, this natural wonder will inspire the artist and nature lover, in all of us. Hidden high in the mountains, the view of the Lake of the Clouds is always breathtaking and is indescribable during color tour season. The lake is fed from the east end by the Carp River Inlet, and the outflow from the western end is the Carp River, which empties into Lake Superior. Drive to the Clouds Overlook at the west terminus, of Michigan Highway M-107. The Lake of the Clouds is located inside the Porcupine Mountains State Park, in Ontonagon County Michigan.

Winter Fun – Ontonagon County, has over 500 miles of hiking, skiing, and snowmobile trails. This is the starting point, for ATV riders, to take the Bill Nicholls multi-use trail. The trail starts at Adventure Mountain, in Greenland, and takes the ATV rider past many old copper mines. This trail also provides remarkable views from high on top of three different trestles, overlooking the Flintsteel and the Firesteel Rivers. The trail continues all the way to South Range, a distance of more than 40 miles.

You will also find a scenic ATV ride from Bergland, in southern Ontonagon County, to Sidnaw. This trail will take you over a trestle that sits high on top of the scenic Agate waterfall. This multi-use trail is also over 40 miles long. Then there is the ATV trail that takes you from Rockland south to Bergland. This trail goes through the forest. From one high hill, there is an amazing view of Lake Superior, which is over 10 miles away.

Along The Way - Spice Vault - Henry's Inn - Paulding Ghost Light

The Konteka is a favorite dining venue in this area, but if you are looking for a pasty, *Henry's Inn* in Rockland, should be on your list. They are using a recipe from three generations back, and the results are mouth-watering. Note that Thursday is pasty day. While in Rockland, stop at the Depot General Store. Inside is a *spice vault,* where you will find spices from all over the world.

The *Paulding Mystery Light*, or *Ghost Light*, has been a subject of wonder and speculation, for several generations. The "ghost light" appears after dark, in and above the wilderness, surrounding Paulding. Reports of the mysterious light began soon after the area began to be settled, during the logging and mining eras. People reported seeing the light in all seasons, and from different areas. The light isn't visible every night and it varies in appearance, with different colors and moving in a variety of directions. Sometimes it seems to move in a straight line. Sometimes the light seems to bounce around the distant hilltops. At other times it seems to drop down into the forest itself. These days, Ghost Light sightings are usually reported from the dead end, on Robbins Road.

Back Roads Lodging - The *The Konteka* has a full restaurant, lounge, bowling, gift shop, and guest rooms. The dining room is famous for the wall of windows on one side. Outside those windows, the staff disposes of kitchen scraps, and huge black bears come charging out of the forest to chow down. It is exciting to be so close to these big *Black Bears*, especially at night under the lights.

www.thekonteka.com – 906-885-5170

Lewiston Getaway

If you are looking for pure sparkling waters, pristine forest trails, and pine scented wilderness air, Lewiston is just the hidden treasure you are seeking. Lewiston, Michigan, is located in the northeast area of Lower Michigan, in the southwest corner of Montmorency County. Less than a 30 minute drive east of I-75, Lewiston has been a favored destination for generations, for those who have discovered the area. After the lumber era, around 1935, the town developed as a resort area, and continues as such today.

Lewiston, Michigan is a nature lovers paradise. The town sits on the shore of East Twin Lake, with more than 40 other lakes nearby. A short drive in any direction, takes you into the forest, or Elk country, or Kirtland's Warbler country. There are numerous hiking and skiing trails in the forests, where the bald eagles live, plus the snow mobile trails are groomed for winter. The combination of natural beauty, and small town hospitality, is hard to resist. If you time your visit just right, *Morel Mushrooms* thrive here, and the *Timbertown Festival,* draws huge crowds, to celebrate the lumbering history of the area.

Day 1 - On The Water - Twin Lakes - Fletcher Flooding
The Twin Lakes are right outside your door, and provide lots of room for fishing, boating, and other water sports. During a five day stay, we fished on a different lake every day. A short drive away is the famous Fletcher Flooding.

Also known as Fletcher Pond, this body of water has something for everyone, except vast sandy beaches. It was created by the construction of a dam, on one branch of the Thunder Bay River. A 9,000 acre shallow water paradise is the result. This is the perfect destination for bird watchers, fishermen, and nature enthusiasts. There are more than 20 osprey nesting platforms. This is one of the largest populations of osprey east of the Mississippi River. The best way to observe them, is from a boat with binoculars. There is nothing quite like seeing an osprey come exploding up out of the lake, after it dives after a fish.

Day 2 - Kirtland's Warbler - Kirtland's Warbler, a member of the wood warbler family, nests in a few counties in Michigan, in Wisconsin, in Ontario. In 1903, Norman A. Wood found the first Kirtland's Warbler nest in Michigan, in Oscoda County. It wasn't until 1996, that any other nests were found, more than 60 miles from this region. Just a few miles south of Lewiston, is Route F-32. That is one drive through Kirtland's Warbler viewing areas. An alternative drive is the Jack Pine Auto Tour.

Day 3 - Elk Country - A half hour north is Atlanta, known as the Elk Capital. If you travel east out of Lewiston a few miles, a paved road leads north, through the forest to Atlanta. Here are the largest areas of undeveloped land, in the entire Lower Peninsula. There are choice trails for ORVs, and snow mobiles, on hundreds of acres of state land. The hiking trails are well maintained, allowing hours of nature hiking. There is an abundance of natural 'candy,' like blueberries, morel mushrooms, raspberries, and blackberries. That means, this is wonderful habitat for a large variety of wildlife like elk, deer, black bear, bobcat, wild turkey, partridge, bald eagle, and pileated wood peckers just to name a few!

Winter Fun - The Curling Club —Buttles Road Trail
There are only a handful of curling facilities, scattered across Michigan. The *Curling Club*, an excellent and modern facility, is located just a block from downtown Lewiston. The interior is beautifully done. They offer two complete courts, and all of the equipment you need to enjoy the sport. The club does have regular hours and events. During the winter, outside groups can rent the club. Rental includes full instruction, all equipment and a fun curling session.

For those who love time on those snow shoes, the *Buttles Road Trail*, just north of town, offers a great mix of wilderness and scenery. The trail is motor free.

Along The Way - It isn't all trails and nature areas in Lewiston. There are fantastic places to eat here as well. Talley's Log Cabin Bar at the main intersection is known to travelers and locals alike. However, for the best burger, it is The Hotel that rates as one of the top three burgers I have found, anywhere in Michigan. The Redwood Steakhouse consistently serves a mouth-watering rib eye steak. Just up the road is the *Garland Resort* with some of the best golf resorts in Northern Michigan.

Also nearby is the tiny town of Lovell's. Folks come to Lewiston for a couple days, just to participate in the Lovell's Bridge Walk. While not as busy as the walk across the Mackinac Bridge, attendees insist it is a lot more fun. The Lovell's bridge spans the north branch of the Au Sable River.

Back Roads Lodging

The *Garland Resort* is a world class golf resort, with a range of lodging options and dining venues, open in warm months.

www.garlandusa.com – 877-442-7526

Ludington Getaway

When sharing stories about Lake Michigan, favorite stunning sunsets are, always included. The shoreline at Ludington, will serve up all of the romantic sunsets you can handle. If you are looking for a quiet stroll, with a heart stopping sunset and the soothing sounds of waves coming ashore, this is the spot. Visitors who arrive by car, drive through downtown, with its cool shops, galleries and restaurants, to get to the shore. Visitors who arrive via the Badger car ferry, cruise in and disembark, right next to Ludington's beautiful art park. Either way, there are miles of sandy beaches and dunes for those sunset walks.

Day 1 - Cool Shops - Maude's Garage - Todd & Brad Reed Gallery – James Street Antiques

Downtown Ludington has excellent parking, so visitors can take a walk to enjoy the really unique shops and galleries, that showcase the works of a vibrant arts community. *Maude's Garage* is difficult to miss. It is right on Ludington Avenue and is the place to find the works of local artists and crafters.

Perhaps the best photographers in Michigan, operate the fantastic *Todd & Brad Reed Gallery,* in downtown Ludington. Todd & Brad Reed have elevated the art of photography to a whole new level. The gallery is full of their incredible images. You will see Michigan in ways you've never even imagined. Reasonably priced originals are for sale, along with their books, prints, and videos.

The James Street Shopping district is the place to go for unique shops, antiques and interesting dining. A stroll down James St. will bring you to Jamesport Center, a late Victorian, six storefront complex. The earliest section was completed in 1890, and was occupied by the Red Andrews Saloon and the Central House Hotel. The jewel of this district is the *Jamesport Brewing Company*.

Day 2 - Historic Attractions - Arts Council Building - Big Sable Point Lighthouse - White Pine Village

In addition to the enormous red Mason County Courthouse, there are a number of historic buildings and destinations around Ludington. One example is the United Methodist Church building, a Gothic style structure built in 1894, now home to the Ludington Area Arts Council.

Another is the *Big Sable Point Lighthouse,* listed on both the state and national registers of historic places. This lighthouse is one of the tallest in Michigan. The black-and-white striped, 112 foot lighthouse, at the Ludington State Park, stands on the shore of Lake Michigan, and remains a testament, to lighthouse keepers of the past. Big Sable Point Lighthouse was honored, as the 2013 Featured Lighthouse of the Year, for the Great Lakes Lighthouse Festival. The Sable Points Lighthouse

Keepers Association maintains the Big Sable Point Lighthouse. It is open for tours daily, from May 1 to October 31.

The historic *White Pine Village* was opened in 1976, by the Mason County Historical Society. Situated on 23 acres, the site boasts more than 25 buildings, and thousands of implements and artifacts, that bring the rich history of the region to life. This museum even has one of the rare Opera Cars, that still exist. The log cabin constructions, and the stone chimneys, will really take you back to the pioneering days, when pine was king in Michigan.

White Pine Village is just a short drive from downtown Ludington. You want to plan for a little extra time here. The site is quite extensive, and there is a lot to see in nearly every building. Exhibits include: Three Log Buildings - Old Fashioned Ice Cream Parlor - Museum of Music - Mason County Sports Hall of Fame - Maritime Museum - Lumbering Museum - Time Museum - Saw Mill - and more.

Day 3 - Shoreline Attractions - Sculpture Park - Scenic Shoreline Drive - Dunes and Beaches

The *Waterfront Sculpture Park* is right between the two marinas, in view of the car ferry dock. Walking along the pathways, you can learn some interesting facts and history, from the nine bronze sculptures that include, children running, fishermen, and women of history. There are five acres to relax in, and watch the S.S. Badger come sailing in, or just enjoy the cool breeze off Pere' Marquette Lake.

Heading for the lake shore, you can spot one of the other lighthouses. The **Ludington Light**, a 57 foot tall steel-plated lighthouse, at the end of the breakwater on the Pere Marquette Harbor. The park and beach access are there as well. Driving north along the lake, will bring visitors to long expanses of **sand dunes** and **secluded beaches,** where watching sunsets is the main pass time. At the north end of the drive, is the **Ludington State Park**. It is considered one of the finest in Michigan, and is where the **Big Sable Lighthouse** is located.

Winter Fun - On New Years Eve, thousands of people gather in Ludington for the **Downtown Ball Drop**.

Manistique Getaway

Manistique has always fascinated visitors, sportsmen, and explorers. Various bands of Indians settled this area. Explorers and missionaries, traveling through, sent back stories of natural beauty, natural beauty that still attracts visitors. The history of Manistique, Michigan is preserved in its architecture, festivals, and museums. Manistique is just 80 miles west of the Mackinac Bridge, on the shore of Lake Michigan.

As soon as you arrive, the bright red lighthouse, out in the sparkling water, will catch your eye. The beach is right across the road from the Gray Wolf Lodge. Marking the passage of the river, through downtown, is the giant, historic water tower. That is the spot where the, one-of-a-kind, Siphon Bridge was located. This area is one of the most historic, and beautiful, in the central upper peninsula. It is still a favorite spot, from which to explore and enjoy, all of the treasures hidden away, in the quiet surrounding forests.

Day 1 - Around Town - Beach Boardwalk - Wine Tasting - Water Tower Museum & Siphon Bridge

Construction on the *Manistique Boardwalk* began in the early 1990s, with several extensions and improvements, in the intervening years. The boardwalk runs almost 2 miles. Beginning at the eastern city limits, it offers breathtaking views of Lake Michigan, and that distinctive red lighthouse. Then it passes under the U. S. Highway 2 bridge, and heads into the downtown district. Along the way users can pause at a fishing pier, walk out to the east breakwater lighthouse, and rest up at the picnic grounds. The *Mackinaw Trail Winery*, has one of its four Michigan Tasting Rooms, near the marina. The winery and tasting room, are part of a family owned business, that continues a long heritage of producing hand-crafted wines. Nearby is the *Upper Crust Cafe*, where the food is fantastic, and the seating is perfect, for watching the boats going by.

It is hard to miss the *Water Tower Museum & Siphon Bridge*, where the historical society has been so effective. The tower, with a capacity of 200,000 gallons, is 200 feet tall in an octagon shape. The upper peninsula has seen a long list of engineering marvels, created during the lumber and mining booms, of previous centuries. One that is unique, perhaps in the world, was the Siphon Bridge in Manistique.

In the early 1900s, the Manistique Pulp and Paper Company, had overcome tremendous obstacles to harness the power of the Manistique River, for their manufacturing facility. Their efforts had included building a reinforced dam, a mill, and a canal, to confine the river. The canal is over 1/2 mile long, with concrete walls, rising above the river. While the canal worked perfectly, to deliver 650,000 gallons of water per hour to the mill wheel, the height of the sides made it nearly impossible, to raise bridges across the canal. The fantastic solution was the Siphon Bridge.

The *Siphon Bridge* was built in 1919. The roadway itself, was as much as 4 feet BELOW the water level. The bridge was supported by water, that was forced under it, using atmospheric pressure. The feed flume was 3,000 feet long and 200 feet wide. The engineering is amazing. This whole project was about like carrying the bridge across the river, in a half-cylinder, set in the water of the canal. Full sets of plans and demonstrations are available at the museum. In its original form, the bridge was listed in "Ripley's Believe It or Not", because the road was actually below the level of the water in the flume.

Day 2 - Historic Sites - Seul Choix Point Lighthouse - Michigan's Boot Hill Cemetery - Baraga Shrine

Architecturally unique, and beautifully designed the *Seul Choix Point Lighthouse,* south of nearby Gulliver, Michigan is really worth the drive, however, part of the road turns to gravel. Pronounced locally, Sis-Shwa, and true French, Sel-Shwa, roughly translated as your "Only Choice." Seul Choix was named by the French, who found that it was the only harbor of refuge, in this part of Lake Michigan. If boats were headed for the Straits of Mackinac, the only choice for safety, was Seul Choix. Seul Choix was the most important fishing station along the north shore of Lake Michigan. This is a very beautiful lighthouse with wonderful colors and lines.

This conical brick light tower, was originally built in 1895, to guide the way for the increasing number of vessels carrying iron ore, that was being shipped out of Escanaba, MI. It stands at 78'9" and produces a lens focal plane 80' above the mean low water level of Lake Michigan. The tower is surmounted by a 10-sided cast iron lantern. The lantern originally held a third order Fresnal lens but is now fitted with a modern airport beacon lens. Tower tours are available, and visitors are welcome to enjoy the surrounding grounds, which include a picnic area, walking paths, and public boat launch.

The origins of the name remain somewhat obscure. Seul Choix Point was supposedly named by French sailors, who found that the protected bay formed by the point, was their "only choice" for shelter, along that stretch of northern Lake Michigan's shoreline. Father William Gagnieur, a scholar and itinerant Jesuit missionary among the Native Americans during the early 1900s claimed, that locals called the point Shishewah, derived from the Ojibwa word Shashoweg, which refers to the "straight line" of the coast. Regardless of the name's origin, today its preferred pronunciation is "Sis-shwa".

Just a few miles east of Manistique is Route 77, which heads north from U.S. 2. That road runs through the Seney Wildlife Sanctuary, to the historic logging town of Seney. A couple miles south of the old railroad depot is a cemetery, full of unmarked and partially marked graves.

We call it *Michigan's Boot Hill.*

Seney, on M-28, is another cross-roads in Michigan. Seney is rich in stories from the lumber era, that most have forgotten. This stretch of highway is what has been described as the most boring stretch of road in Michigan, but its history is anything but boring. The immigrant lumberjacks followed the vanishing forests north, and many simply disappeared in this vast wilderness. At one time, characters named "Stub Foot" O'Donnell, Frying Pan Mag, and "Pump Handle" Joe were part of the local scene. These guys and others, gave Seney the reputation as the toughest spot in the Upper Peninsula. Few remember the epic fist fight between "Wild Hughie" Logan and "Killer" Shea. Ears were bitten and eyes gouged, but it was a draw in the end. Tales of gambling, corruption, and even slavery brought the area known as the Ram's Pasture under investigation in the late 1800s. The stilt houses that were constructed, due to the wetlands, are gone. The gambling and drinking houses are gone. The old cemetery, and the graves marked "Unknown", are still there.

If you continue west on M-28 to M-94, and head south back toward Manistique, you can find the *Baraga Shrine* near Indian Lake. The shrine includes a chapel, Indian dwellings, and other buildings, open to the public. The Indians replaced the first chapel with a larger one, in 1833. Records suggest that the chapel may have existed until 1873. Based on historical information, the Indian

Lake mission was rebuilt in the early 1980s, on the original mission's site. Frederick Baraga was called "The Apostle of the Ottawas and Chippewas." He built a number of missions in the Upper Peninsula, including a famous one at L'Anse.

Day 3 - Nature Areas - Mirror of Heaven - Rainey Wildlife Area

Kitch-Iti-Kipi (cold big water), or The Big Spring, was a sacred place to the native inhabitants of this area. One of the names they gave it was the "***Mirror of Heaven***". Kitch-Iti-Kipi is the largest spring in Michigan, at 300 feet by 175 feet. Fed by more than 20 springs, it is refreshed continuously, with crystal-clear water. More than 10,000 gallons a minute gush up, from the limestone bed.

There are several legends associated with the 40+ foot deep pool. One is, that in the past, some of the springs would spout columns of water high into the air. Another legend may explain the pattern at the bottom of the spring that some say, resembles a beautiful Native American maiden. While her lover was absent, she was trying to elude an unwanted suitor, and dove into the spring. The magical qualities of the waters transformed her into a white deer. From this event came the taboo, among native tribes, against the killing of white deer. There are other legends, including the idea that the waters were lethal, since they don't freeze in winter, and no frogs or turtles live in the pool.

The "Big Spring", Kitch-Iti-Kipi, is located just west of Manistique, at Palms Book State Park. Go downtown, then go across the river where the old siphon bridge is and follow the signs. Alternately, go west of Manistique on U.S. 2 to Thompson, take M-149 north for 12 miles to the park. There is plenty of parking, and it is a short walk to the spring, along a paved path. A self-operated observation raft takes visitors across the spring, so you can view the underwater features. There is a State Park fee.

Another favorite nature area is the 100+ acre *Rainey Wildlife Area*. A hiking trail passes through mixed hardwoods and conifers. There are boardwalks for the wet areas, and eventually you reach an elevated platform, that is excellent for bird-watching. The platform has a barrier-free ramp, that reaches mid-level, and offers a scenic view of the sedge meadow and open water wetlands. The trail crosses Smith Creek, which flows through a patterned fen, to Indian Lake. This area is popular for bird-watching. Warblers are found here, and it is not difficult to find nesting eagles. Be sure to bring your camera during fall color tour season.

To get there from U.S. 2 in Manistique, drive north through town on M-94, about 5 miles, to Dawson Road. Turn left (west), and proceed 1.5 miles to an access road, that goes north to the site parking lot. There are no facilities at this area, so be prepared for spending some time in a fairly remote wilderness.

Along The Way - Pictured Rocks - Fayette

Manistique is on Lake Michigan, yet the ***Pictured Rocks*** National Lakeshore, and the fantastic boat tour out along the cliffs of Lake Superior, is less than an hour away. You can drive up, have lunch, take the breath-taking boat tour, and be back before dinner time. The part of the Lakeshore called ***Pictured Rocks,*** got its name from the 15 miles of colorful sandstone cliffs, northeast of Munising. The cliffs have been sculpted by wind, water, and ice into spectacular formations, including caves and arches. The cliffs, up to 200 feet above the lake, exhibit fantastic colors depending on time of day and angle of the sun. The boat tour only takes a couple hours, is informative, entertaining, and gets you up close to the cliffs, huge formations, and waterfalls. During the boat trip, you will discover a very old lighthouse on Grand Island, waterfalls, natures water slide, beaches, and sand dunes. The tour boats get you very close to some of the formations, like the "Battleship", and a towering archway that has been formed. If you decide to spend a full day, you can kayak out to the cliffs, go to Mosquito Falls, or visit Miner's Castle, with its interpretive center.

The "ghost town" of ***Fayette*** is on the Garden Peninsula, on Snail Shell Harbor. Until the late 1890s, this was one of the most productive iron-smelting businesses in the

Upper Peninsula. Now a State Park, Fayette is a restored village, including 22 historic buildings, museum exhibits, and the visitor center. The park is only open in the summer months.

Winter Fun - Manistique has a Sno-Fest, ice fishing contests, and cross-country skiing. Just out of town on the west side of Indian Lake, the Indian Lake Pathways Ski Trail, has trails ranging from just under a mile in length, to twenty three miles. The Rainey Wildlife Area is considered one of the best for snowshoeing. There are hundreds of miles of groomed trails leading off in every direction regardless of where you start. The "***Thunder Bowl***" has become a must visit playground for snowmobiles. It is the site of an abandoned ski hill, and attracts traditional sledders, as well as snowmobiles. The "Thunder Bowl" is 22 miles northwest of Manistique on Thunder Lake.

Back Roads Lodging - The ***Gray Wolf Lodge*** maintains a private beach in case you just want to relax. Access to the boardwalk is nearby.

www.visitmanistique.com – 906-341-2410

PIERCE

CEDAR

CREEK

INSTITUTE

IS

A

QUIET

PLACE

NO

MOTORS

ALLOWED

ON

THE

TRAILS

Michigan Prairie Getaway

Michigan has only a few small remnants of its original prairie grasslands remaining. The wildflowers, songbirds, and other wildlife that inhabited those prairies, and nearby fens, have become scarce as well. Those seeking great stands of tamarack trees, rolling hills, and deep trillium-filled canyons, usually think, "up north". There is another place where the prairie still lives. ***Pierce Cedar Creek Institute*** is a West Michigan destination, where more than 660 acres of pristine wilderness, are being preserved. Over seven miles of groomed trails, beckon the visitor to explore this unique environment.

The view, looking out from the Visitor Center, is a mix of broad prairies, deep ravines, and rolling forested hills. One can just glimpse the nature trails, wetlands, a kettle lake, and constructed prairies. Not far from the Visitor Center, on a separate parcel of Institute property, is a deep canyon with a spring fed stream, that fills with wildflowers at winter's end, when the trilliums are in bloom. It is accessible on scheduled guided tours, in the spring.

The grounds of Pierce Cedar Creek Institute include seven different trails, each of which has its own special characteristics. One trail has wetlands and retention ponds, as its main features. Another passes through a fen, an oak forest with huge trees, a pasture/prairie, and a view of Brewster Lake. Yet another trail runs through a sand prairie and is characterized by being more primitive than the others. Walkers, hikers, skiers, and snowshoe enthusiasts will find trails that match their fitness and skill level.

The trails are quiet. There are no motorized vehicles, no snowmobiles, no bicycles, not even horses, none are allowed. There is no fishing, hunting, or camping, but there is solitude. You can wander through the trees, more than twenty varieties are growing here, including giant beech trees, American hornbeam, and mature black walnut. Enjoy the flora but collecting is not allowed. Everything is to be enjoyed and preserved. There are wildflowers, wild turkeys, and deer. Needless to say, songbirds abound.

Day 1 - Short Trails - Getting to the Institute, you'll take a winding road through the wetlands and a tamarack fen. If it is autumn, the tamaracks will be golden, and the hardwoods will be ablaze with color. After check in, explore the Visitor Center, with its quarterly art exhibits, gift shop, and an extraordinary collection of antique clocks. Linger a while, there will still be time to enjoy a couple of the short trails, at the very least.

Lupine Trail (Green Trail) - 0.4 miles - The primary features of this trail, are retention ponds, panoramic views, a small section of open forest, and a wetland dominated by skunk cabbage. ***Black Walnut Trail*** (Loop Trail) – 0.2 miles - This trail provides wonderful panoramic views of the Visitor Center, through a walnut and black cherry grove.

Day 2 - Two Trails - *Old Farm Trail* (Orange Trail) - 1.3 miles - One of the easiest trails to hike, it is great for an early morning walk. It provides both open field and forested views. The prairie loop provides a closer view of the prairie. *Tall Grass Prairie Trail* (Yellow Trail) – 0.4 mile - This is a shortcut to the middle of the Blue Trail. One of the beautiful, constructed wildflower prairies is on the west side of the trail.

Day 3 - Two Trails - *Beech Maple Ridge Trail* (Blue Trail) - 1.75 miles - This trail winds through a second-growth forest with mature oaks, beeches, maples, a section of swamp forest, and a fen. On the east loop, one can spot a beech tree, with branches that actually form a closed loop. Further on is the recently added boardwalk, through a wetland, leading back to the Visitors Center. *Cedar Creek Trail* (White Trail) - 0.9 mile - This trail runs through a sand prairie, with a great view of the pure running water of Cedar Creek, and then loops back to the Blue Trail. It is a primitive trail, and somewhat more strenuous, than the other trails. Blue and white trail markers, along with white markings on some trees, help point the way.

Special Times & Programs - Visitors can learn about restoring and preserving natural habitats, and enjoy the programs, held in these earth-friendly buildings, or out on the trail. For a calendar of upcoming events, visit www.cedarcreekinstitute.org or call (269)721-4190. Information is also available on bird and butterfly gardening, prairie management, wildlife tracking, the solstices, and much more, in the gift shop. Restrooms are available at the Visitor Center, from dawn to dusk. When the wildflowers bloom in spring, a pre-scheduled guided tour, to the wildflower ravine, is available by registration only. On the second Sunday of November each year, there is a *Holiday Gift Show.* It is a one-day event, featuring dozens of the most talented crafters in mid-Michigan. Winter also turns the entire 661 acres into a wonderland. Hiking, cross-country skiing, and snowshoeing are all ways to make your way along the tree-lined trails through the silent forest.

Directions: Please note: you will have to navigate gravel roads to get to the Institute. Pierce Cedar Creek Institute is located at 701 W. Cloverdale Rd., south of Hastings in Barry County. M-37 runs from Grand Rapids to Battle Creek. West Cloverdale Road heads west from M-37 just north of Dowling. M-43 runs from Kalamazoo to Lansing with West Cloverdale Road heading east just north of Delton. Look for the directional road signs when approaching West Cloverdale Road.

Around The Area - Gilmore Car Museum - Otis Farm Bird Sanctuary - Bellevue Drive In

A few miles south of the Institute, is the *Gilmore Car*

Museum , which is considered one of the Nation's best car museums. The museum houses 300+ cars, many of which are extremely rare. There is a classic Duesenberg, an unusual 1948 Tucker, and many others. The museum is open every day, year-round, and is at 6865 W Hickory Rd, Hickory Corners, MI.

Bird lovers will want to include an excursion to the ***Otis Farm Bird Sanctuary***. According to their literature, *"Otis Sanctuary is adjacent to the Globally Important Bird Area, Barry State Game Area, which recognizes critical habitat for Cerulean Warblers. The 128 acre bird sanctuary hosts rolling fields, mature forest, expansive marshland, a trout stream, kettle hole marshes, and several springs"*. For bird watchers, this is an opportunity to catalog a siting of the rare ***Cerulean Warbler*** in their bird diary. The sanctuary is at 3960 Havens Road Hastings, MI.

Bellevue Drive In - All that hiking on the Institute nature trails, can build an appetite. In the summer months, a short drive east, will bring you to Bellevue and the old-style drive-in restaurant. Car hops take your order at your car, from the huge old-fashioned billboard style menu, or you can relax at outdoor picnic tables. You can get Coney Dogs and Root Beer Floats just like in the old days, but don't miss the onion rings. They are the best. Another favorite eatery is the ***Walldorff Brew Pub & Bistro*** in Hastings, which is only about 10 minutes away. Lots of cool shops line main street, and there is an excellent pawn shop for bargain hunters

.

Back Roads Lodging - The *Lodging at Pierce Cedar Creek* is just as unique as the surrounding nature areas. Rooms are available at very reasonable rates. Visitors will be responsible for their own meals and housekeeping. Check-in time is 3 pm and check-out is at 11 am. Reservations are required, and lodging is subject to availability.

www.cedarcreekinstitute.org – 269-721-4291

Nahma Getaway

This getaway explores three small peninsulas. Michigan is defined by two major peninsulas, the upper and the lower. The Great Lakes surround most of the state, and the waters create inlets, bays, and smaller peninsulas. If you make your way to a small peninsula, on the northern shore of Big Bay De Noc, you will discover Nahma, Michigan, the *Nahma Inn*, and begin to explore three of these lesser peninsulas.

There are three roads that lead into Nahma off U.S. Highway 2, and each is a short scenic drive in its own right. I call this the Nahma Peninsula, though I doubt it has been named that formally. Nahma was a mill town along the north side of Lake Michigan. The town and mill were established as early as 1856, when it gained its first post office. According to Michigan Place Names, Nahma is an Indian word for sturgeon. The middle road into town skirts along the Sturgeon River.

Day 1 - Nahma Peninsula - The Inn - Christine's Gallery - The Burner - Marsh Trail

Both the town of Nahma, and the peninsula, are very small, but there is an art gallery, a golf course, fishing, parks and a hiking trail, the unique Nahma Inn, and the old General Store building. The *Nahma Inn* offers lodging that is a step back in time. All rooms are on the second floor, which is reached by stairs. The venue is from a simpler time with small clean rooms, some with private baths and some with shared baths. Guests gather in the dining room or tavern for great food, and to enjoy the impromptu musical performances, that are liable to break out at any time.

The creations of local artists are on display at *Christine's Gallery*. The work from many talented Upper Michigan artists can be enjoyed here. Exhibits include fine arts, crafts, photography, and all sorts of artistic gifts. Christine's studio offers instructional events to help you in different areas of the arts. Visitors should come hungry with an appetite for art and ice cream!

Between the Inn and the Gallery is the old *General Store* building. The Bay De Noquet Lumber Company was headquartered in Nahma, and built the railroad, the burner, and the company store. The store is closed now, but still contains items that were on the shelves when the company closed down, more than 50 years ago. The television program, "American Pickers", visited the store and the video of that visit can be seen at the inn. If you are lucky, you might get to go in, and "pick" the treasures that are still inside. The lumber company produced so much product that disposing of the sawdust became a problem. Unlike some companies that simply dumped the waste into Lake Michigan, this one built *"the burner"*, a gigantic tower to burn the waste. The huge structure is now fallen on the shoreline just south of the Inn.
North of town hikers and bird watchers can explore the

Nahma Marsh Trail. This is a fun trail near the Sturgeon River, in the Hiawatha National Forest. Ruffled Grouse, whitetail deer, and sand hill cranes are just a few of the native animals you may encounter. Less than half a mile long, the trail once crept under a dense cedar forest, but a windstorm in 1997 leveled the trees, leaving hikers today with broad vistas of the marsh. The trail ends at a two-tiered viewing platform, where an assortment of wetland wildlife can be seen. Rest areas with benches are spaced every 200 feet or so, along the trail.

The trail is regaining its natural appearance as the forest heals from the effects of the windstorm. If you go in the spring, especially early May, you might spot eagles. During an afternoon visit in the first week of May 2012, I encountered two pairs of Bald Eagles. Based on their aggressive behavior I would guess that they were nesting nearby.

Day 2 - Garden Peninsula - Fayette – Fairport

The east road out of Nahma runs past the golf course to Highway 2. A few miles east on 2 will bring visitors to Garden Corners, and Route 183. Turning to the right, that is south, on Route 183, takes travelers down through the Garden Peninsula to Fayette.

The "ghost town" of ***Fayette*** is on Snail Shell Harbor. Until the late 1890s, this was one of the most productive iron-smelting businesses in the Upper Peninsula. There were huge furnaces, an extensive dock, and several kilns in operation. Nearly 500 people lived and worked here for 20+ years, in a town that existed just to produce pig iron. Now a State Park, Fayette is a restored village including 22 historic buildings, museum exhibits, and the visitor center.

The grounds are an easy walk and the surrounding scenery is really breathtaking. You can get an excellent orientation and overview of this area at the welcome center. They have a model of the entire site, and plenty of documentation. The park is only open in the summer months.

Fairport has operated as a fishing port for hundreds of years. If you continue south from Fayette to the end of the road, there is Fairport. Little more than a fishing site now, there are fine views of the Summer and Poverty Islands. Some of the nearby Farmer's Markets will have fresh White Fish from these waters, during the season. Large populations of Menominee Indians had occupied the Garden Peninsula before European settlers arrived. So many acres had been cultivated, that the peninsula was named "Garden".

Day 3 - Stonington Point Peninsula - Bald Eagles - Scenic Drive - Stonington Point Lighthouse and Monarch Butterflies

The center road out of Nahma runs along the Sturgeon River. There are a couple of turn-offs, that lead to fishing spots, where you may very likely encounter **Bald Eagles** diving for fish in the river. When you reach U.S. Highway 2, go across on to Route H-13. This road runs straight north through pristine forests for about 35 miles where you turn left on Route 94. Continue about 15 miles and turn south on Route 67, which leads to Trenary, where that fantastic Trenary Toast is toasted. You can find bags of it in local groceries. Just dip it into your coffee and get ready for a real treat. Get on Route 41 south, back to Highway 2. Head east again, and in just a couple miles, you will see a sign that says "Stonington Point". It is a paved road for the first 17 miles. You can park, and walk the last gravel mile, or drive right to the point.

Stonington Peninsula Point is a pleasant day trip with trees, picnic areas, and a three story abandoned lighthouse that is open for visitors. You can climb to the top of the lighthouse and look down the lake toward Green Bay. This is a quiet spot all year round. The hike from the car park to the point in the winter months is just gorgeous. During the fall of every year, a rare event takes place here. Monarch Butterflies gather by the thousands. They may not be there on one day and then, a couple days later, the trees will be festooned with butterflies. For many years the DNR received reports of strange twisting clouds high above Lake Michigan, called in by folks on color tours around the Leelanau peninsula, which is south of here across Lake Michigan. The reports were generally dismissed as having no validity; "too much time spent wine tasting" perhaps. Then the age of digital cameras and hand-held video arrived. It was discovered that the unusual clouds were real, and that they were actually enormous flocks of Monarch butterflies. Every autumn, during the last two weeks of August and the first two weeks of September, the Monarchs gather at Stonington Point. They pause here until the winds are right for the migration flight, south across Lake Michigan, Green Bay, and on to their winter grounds in Mexico.

Winter Fun - You can take a snowshoe walk along the Marsh Trail, or for the adventurous, take a day trip to the *Eben Ice Caves*. The Eben Ice caves are part of the 4,000 plus acre Rock River Wilderness area of the Hiawatha National Forest. This is a fairly rough hike and the last half can be treacherous. After you park, it is about a quarter mile across a field, and into the woods to the river gorge. Then a steep, slippery hike down to the river is followed by another short hike, and then, back up the cliffs to reach the ice caves. The caves are formed each winter by water seeping out of the cliff side and freezing into giant vertical sheets of ice. You can actually walk behind the cascades of ice into the caves. In spite of the difficulty and lack of services, this is well worth it. Take U.S.41 north to 67 to Chatham, Michigan and Route 94 to Hwy 365 aka Eben Rd to 388 Frey Rd. Follow the yellow signs, avoid the yellow snow.

Along The Way - If you can plan your trip for June you

can attend the ***Nahma Music Festival***. Every June, musicians and artists, gather at the Township Hall and Park Grounds. Music is the thing, but there is delicious food, and fun as well. The Nahma Inn isn't open for breakfast. Just drive over to Rapid River, and go to Jack's, awesome breakfast and giant cinnamon rolls.

Back Roads Lodging – The Nahma Inn

www.nahmainn.com - 906-644-2486

ALCONA

COUNTY

CREATED

THE

FIRST

QUILT

BLOCK

TRAIL

IN

MICHIGAN

Northern Sunrise Side Getaway

The Lake Huron coastline is known as the "Sunrise Side" of Michigan. The "Sunrise Side" extends from the Mackinac Bridge, in the north, all the way to Port Huron, in the south. One of the most beautiful sections of the "Sunrise Side", is in Alcona County, where Harrisville, Michigan is found. Harrisville is home to the original Michigan Quilt Block Trail, Harmony Weekend, the second largest arts and crafts street fair in Michigan, Negwegon State Park with its wilderness trails and mysteries, a famous Wine and Food festival, wineries, historic lighthouses, and on and on.

Day 1 - Scenic Drives - This region of Michigan has preserved the look and feel of times gone by, with deep silent forests, fantastic lake views, and unmatched natural beauty. Two scenic drives will give the visitor a sense of what can be found here. The ***Quilt Block Drive*** meanders all over the county. When approaching Harrisville, you will see huge quilt blocks, mounted on barns and other historic structures. You can tour nearly the entire county on this drive. It is so popular, that small quilt blocks, now adorn many of the local businesses. A map is available at businesses, in downtown Harrisville.

About eleven miles south of town you can find the ***River Road***, one of two National Scenic Byways, in Michigan. This drive starts at Lake Huron, in downtown Oscoda, and follows the Au Sable River all the way to Route 65.

This drive is gorgeous any time of year with several places where stopping is a must, including scenic overlooks of the river, the awesome Iargo Springs, and the Lumberman's Monument, to name just a few. This whole drive is a favorite color tour, when autumn arrives. At Route 65, turn north, and enjoy the winding road through the forest for about ten miles. You will pass through Glennie and get to Route 72. Go east back to Harrisville.

Day 2 - Nature Areas - Much of this region is within the Huron National Forest, so nature areas are all around. The Harbor of Refuge, in Harrisville, is one of the most beautiful on Lake Huron. Lake Hubbard, and the Alcona Dam Pond, are favorites with boaters and fishermen. Almost anywhere you go, there are nicely groomed hiking trails. This part of the Sunrise Side has two of the most unique nature areas anywhere in Michigan, *Iargo Springs* and *Negwegon State Park*.

Iargo Springs is found out along the River Road. Iargo Springs is easily one of the most beautiful, and least known, spots in northeast Michigan. Far down the cliff side, are pools of pristine spring waters, that have been used, and revered, since prehistory. The pools are broad, and the water is so clear that you don't realize that it is several feet deep in places. Revered as a sacred place by natives, marveled at by explorers, discovered and rediscovered, these magical springs will remain in your memory, and call you back again and again! Being at the springs in the quiet glade, and hearing the cry of a Bald Eagle overhead, is a great experience.

When you visit Iargo Springs you will need to be prepared to handle the steps, some 300 of them, take your time. Iargo Springs is presented as a Michigan interpretive site. There are minimal facilities, good parking, and an information kiosk. The Lumbernan's Monument is nearby.

Negwegon State Park - We think of camping and toasted marshmallows, when we think of state parks in Michigan. Most of our State Parks are convenient places to take a camper. They provide facilities, showers, and beautiful camp sites in the trees. There are a few that are more rustic, and one, Neqwegon State Park, is one of the only unimproved parks left.

The park is reached by land, after driving along a very rough sand trail, for several miles. It is actually easier to get to the park by canoe or kayak. There is a gravel parking lot at the entrance, you can use the nearby comfort facilities, and there is an artesian well flowing so you can fill your canteen. No vehicles are allowed in the park, so you hike to your campsite. There are only four campsites, with rustic facilities, spread along the two mile main trail. The northernmost campsite, #4, is in view of the Bird Islands. Each campsite has its own private beach on Lake Huron.

Between campsite 3 and campsite 4 the trail splits. The

branch to the right will take you across a prairie to campsite 4. Exploring the prairie will reveal an old stone water well, and the foundations of an old cabin. The story is told that during the last century, a free black man lived here, all alone, and disappeared without a trace. Hike into this remote place during the winter, and you will wonder how anyone could survive in this isolated location, 100 years ago, all alone.

If you take the trail to the left, before you enter the prairie, you can hike for a couple more miles as the trail loops back toward the parking area. You will cross a small stream, a hundred yards or so, along the left branch. Down that stream, deep in the swamp, are old stone walls and cairns, built long ago by parties unknown.

Directions - Negwegon State Park is located on the shores of Lake Huron a few miles north of Black River. Take Route 23 north from Harrisville and follow the signs to Black River. Route 23 and the Black River road are paved. The road to the park is gravel and sand and can be rather rough.

Day 3 - Historic Places - Historic sites include the Craftmakers Cabin, the Bailey One Room Schoolhouse, the Lincoln Train Depot Museum, and others. Two unique destinations are the Lumberman's Monument and the Sturgeon Point Lighthouse.

The ***Lumberman's Monument*** was erected in 1931, as a memorial to the lumbermen, who harvested Michigan's giant white pines in the 1800s. The 14-foot bronze statue overlooks the beautiful Au Sable River ("River of Sand"). The three figures represent various stages of the historic lumbering operation.

In the center, the "timber cruiser" holds a compass. To his left, a "sawyer" holds an ax and cross-cut saw. On the right, is the "river rat" using a "peavey". Outside, visitors view the Lumberman's Monument statue up close, take pictures, and enjoy the overlook of the Au Sable River, a beauty that draws people back to its banks year after year. In the outdoor exhibit area, large scale replicas of a Rollway, logjam, comfort station, wanigan, hands-on peavey, and log stamping areas, add to the story of the lumbermen. The outdoor displays and trails highlight the "River Rats", and driving logs to the sawmills.

The ***Sturgeon Point Lighthouse*** was built in 1869, and has been in continuous service for 128 years. A museum, on the grounds, hold examples of boats, rudders, and Lake Huron equipment. The gift shop has plenty of cool items, and there is excellent rock and shell hunting along the shore. The keepers house is now a museum, and is open Memorial Day - mid September. In addition to that, the old ***Bailey One Room School*** is also on adjacent grounds. After you tour the buildings, consider a walk from the Sturgeon Point Lighthouse, out to the point. **Winter Fun** – The trails that wind through these pristine woods, are perfect for cross country skiing and hiking. The Reid Lake area has easily accessible trails. Just south of the county line, are the Corsair Trails, that are a winter favorite.

Back Roads Lodging - The ***Lake Huron Inn*** takes pampering their guests seriously. Private jetted tubs in every suite, set the tone for romance. Nothing is more beautiful, or breathtaking, than the stunning sunrises and moon rises over Lake Huron, enjoyed from the private beach.

www.lakehuroninn.com – 989-734-5331

Pentwater Getaway

Pentwater, Michigan is an historic village, situated at the outlet of the Pentwater River, between Pentwater Lake and Lake Michigan. This quaint village has gorgeous tree-lined streets, charming victorian homes, and cottages. Downtown Pentwater invites you to stroll along the street, enjoying the wide variety of unique shops. You can pause on the village green, where Thursday evening band concerts, have been a tradition for more than 50 years.

Day 1 - Around Town - Perhaps the best part of Pentwater is the traditional downtown area with unique shops, historic architecture, and good food. The ***Brown Bear*** has long been famous for their burger. Bicycling is a great way to tour the area and see the great architecture and gorgeous gardens. ***Mears Park*** is nearby for beach goers, and the waterfront is just a block from the main street. Just north of town, is the scenic Lake Shore Drive, where Bortell's has been serving up the best fried and smoked fish in the area, for 5 generations.

Day 2 - Nature Areas - Pentwater Michigan is known as a favorite summer destination to some, but it is also a great place for a Michigan winter getaway. The ***Pentwater Pathways*** are gorgeous for a summer hike. However, they are really perfect, for winter cross country skiing. There are miles of trails and paths, within the Pere Marquette State Forest. The paths can be enjoyed year round. They are great for hiking and mountain biking in spring, summer, and fall, and skiing in the winter. The Pathways trail system includes four loops, totaling 15 miles, with beginner to advanced trails. The trails cover mostly soft rolling hills, which are heavily wooded with abundant wildlife.

From downtown Pentwater, just south of town, turn west on Long Bridge Road. Cross the bridge and turn left on Wayne Road. Watch for a marked turn, onto a gravel road to the right, in about a mile. The parking area is a widened space in the road, 0.3 mile in. You will notice the bench, at the entrance to the trail system, on your right. No motorized vehicles are allowed. The trail was built for ski use and is groomed in the winter. Please snowshoe beside groomed trails rather than in them.

Lavender Labyrinth - Labyrinths are found around the world. They have been constructed since ancient times, and there is a truly beautiful one, right here in Michigan. The Lavender Labyrinth covers several acres and is constructed of living lavender. The Labyrinth is on the grounds of the **Cherry Point Farm**, in the area of Oceana County known as Little Point Sable. Unlike a maze, a labyrinth is a continuous circuit and you cannot get lost. Pilgrims entering the great cathedrals of France, during the middle ages, walked the labyrinths inlaid in the cathedral floor, to prepare them for the sacred experience they were about to participate in.

The Lavender Labyrinth is open to everyone and is

usually in full bloom in July and August. It is a perfect place to walk amid lavender, rocks, and wildflowers. There is no charge, and reservations are not needed. Even if you don't have the hour, it is worth taking a look, just to enjoy the sheer beauty of the labyrinth. The labyrinth is on the grounds of the Cherry Point Farm. The address is 9600 West Buchanan Road, Shelby, MI 49455.

Day 3 - Historic Places - The *Pentwater Historical Society* preserves the history of the area at it's museum. The museum is housed in the old First Baptist Church building, an important historic structure. The transformation of the church into a historical museum was a monumental undertaking, for which the Historical Society, is rightfully proud. It not only created a focal point, designed to strengthen, preserve, and share the values of the community, but also preserved one of the oldest historic buildings in Pentwater.

Just six miles away, is the *Hart Historic District*. The downtown Hart Historic District contains the most historical buildings and collections, in Oceana County, and it was created by volunteers! The district is located in downtown Hart, on the edge of Chippewa Creek, in an old business section on the site of the Centennial Northern Market Chesapeake Ohio Railroad deadhead. Several historical collections are displayed, at the corner of Washington and Union Streets, four blocks east of the stoplight. Wandering through this district, of historic buildings and attractions, you will step back 150 years into the past.

Winter Fun - The *Pentwater Pathways* are excellent for cross country skiing. Winter Fest is an annual celebration with a Broomball Tournament, Hart Lake Fishing Tournament, Snow Putt Putt Golf, and a Polar Plunge into the frozen lake.

Port Huron Getaway

One of the oldest settlements in Michigan, Port Huron has everything one could hope for, in an urban getaway. There are more than 30 buildings with unique architecture, not the least of which, is the Carnegie Museum. Downtown runs along Military Street, with structures from the 1800s, all along the way. While most of the attractions are in town, nearly everything here is connected to the St. Clair River, and the Great Lakes. That is where you find the Fort Gratiot Lighthouse, and a working lightship.

Day 1 - Taking The Tours - One way to get an overview of what there is to see, and to get a sense of local history, is to take a couple of tours. One by land, the Blue Water Trolley, takes you on a one hour tour around town. Their tour map lists more than forty points of interest, including a stunning view of the Blue Water Bridges, spanning the river over to Canada. The other, by water, is the river cruise, aboard the Huron Lady II. The trip lasts about an hour and a half. The cruise runs from the dock to Marysville, then to Lake Huron, going beneath the Blue Water Bridges. It is a great way to tour the waterfronts of Port Huron, and Sarnia, on the Canadian side.
Another option is to enjoy the Blue Water River Walk, with its gorgeous views, and informative signage. You can get to the paved walk from Vantage Point, which is also a good place to relax and watch the giant ships go by, on one of the busiest waterways in the world.

Day 2 - Historical Museum - Lightship

The Port Huron Museum is actually a group of museums, each with a distinct purpose, and character. The Carnegie Center is the main component of the group. The building on Sixth St. was built in 1902, to serve as the Port Huron Public Library, as part of the Andrew Carnegie Library Construction project. The architectural styles of Carnegie Libraries across Michigan are unique and beautiful. At one point, the building was to be demolished, but local volunteers saved this magnificent structure. Nothing like these libraries is being built today.

The Main Museum houses thousands of objects, documents, and photographs. Among the exhibits, is the largest collection of model ships, in Michigan. With that exhibit, is a reconstructed, full size, "hands-on" Pilot House, from a Great Lakes freighter. The ship's wheel turns, the lights flash, and the whistles blow, great fun. Then there is the Whiting-Moore Home paneling. The exhibit is a replica of a parlor, from a Victorian Era home. The exhibit has the usual examples of furniture, clothing, and artwork, but it also has the paneling, and the fireplace it surrounds. Rare as it is beautiful, the hand-carved wall paneling and fireplace mantle, are the kind of craftsmanship, that few if any artisans, could produce today. This is not modern laminate. This is solid wood, oak I think, that was fashioned into a wall treatment, and a remarkable work of art. Local history is also preserved through photographs, artifacts, and stories, from the first

Native Americans in the Blue Water Area, to the ground breaking medical advancements that took place in Port Huron.

On the grounds of the main museum, is an authentic German log house. Visitors and students can learn what life was like, for pioneers of the Michigan wilderness. Either during a scheduled demonstration, or during Pioneer Days, visitors learn about making soup and cornbread over an open fire, using a butter churn, dipping candles, and writing with a feather quill pen, among other activities.

The *Lightship Huron*, played a vital role in protecting ships, on their way into and out of Lake Huron, via the St. Clair River. About 6 miles north of Port Huron, is a sandy area in Lake Huron, known as Corsica Shoals. Essentially a big sandbar, Corsica Shoals presents a real danger to be avoided. Areas like this were often too deep, expensive, or otherwise impractical, for the construction of a permanent lighthouse. Lightships, like the Huron, provided the answer. She is a floating lighthouse and was stationed at the shoals for more than three decades.

The Huron displayed her light, equipped with a Fresnel lens, from atop a 42 foot mast. During periods of fog, the ship sounded a fog signal, and broadcast a radio beacon. Over the years the fog signals changed, and included bells, whistles, trumpets, sirens, and horns. Early on the foghorn was steam powered. Later the foghorn blast was produced with compressed air. The Huron sounded her fog horn in 3 second blasts, every 30 seconds. The sound was distinctive and was known locally as "Old B.O.".

The crew of 11 or 12 men manned the ship out on the shoal in all weathers. Their shifts amounted to 3 weeks on and 1 week off. During those 3 weeks, the crew remained on the ship, 24 hours per day. The lightship was completely self-contained, with every necessity provided for, so she could stay on station to guide shipping through the channel into and out of the lake.

The *Lightship Huron* is now a most unique museum in Port Huron. She is permanently moored in Pine Grove Park, on the St. Clair River. There is a fascinating and informative tour, that provides visitors a view of every part of the ship, including "the hole". The demonstration of the function of the Fresnel lens is particularly interesting. The details covered, such as the "fiddle board" on the officers dining room table, the 500 foot anchor chain, the "air conditioning system", and the collection of artifacts bring it all to life. On top of all that, there is a live camera feed of the bottom of the river. Sometimes you can see fish passing by and, if you are very lucky, you might even see a sturgeon. The Huron was dedicated as a National Historic Landmark in 1990.

Day 3 - Lighthouse - Edison Depot - Ice Museum - Fort Gratiot was established in 1814, to guard the juncture of Lake Huron and the St. Clair River. As commercial shipping and other water traffic grew in the early 1800s, Congress approved funds to build the first lighthouse in

Michigan, the second on the entire Great Lakes. The original structure was built near where the first Blue Water Bridge stands today. Things didn't go well for this first lighthouse. The location was not good, and the construction techniques employed, were not much better. In 1828 cracks began to appear in the walls, and the tower began to sag. During a violent storm, in September of that year, the tower sustained additional damage, and the whole thing collapsed in November.

Construction on a new lighthouse began almost immediately. By 1861, a tower more than 80 feet tall and 25 feet in diameter, was completed. The construction techniques employed were much better. The new tower even survived the devastating storms of 1913. A protective retaining wall was added, and the lighthouse was ready to grow into the full light station that exists today. The light is fully automated, flashing every 15 seconds, with a range of 16 miles.

The Lighthouse and station are part of the Port Huron Museum complex. Programs are offered explaining wave action, the science of the light featuring the prism of the Fresnel lens, and a hands on description, of the day to day activities of the early lighthouse keepers. Tours of the lighthouse and keeper residence are available, and there is an excellent gift shop on the grounds.

Along The Way - SandFest - The Blue Water SandFest is the "Masters Level, Michigan State Championships".

The Blue Water SandFest hosts Michigan's only Master sand sculpting, and Advanced Amateur competition/festival. This three day event is held at the foot of the Fort Gratiot Lighthouse, along the beautiful beaches of Lake Huron, over the 4th of July weekend. Event Activities: Master Sand Sculpting (State Championships) Contest, Advanced Amateur (State Championships) Contest, Amateur Contest, Live Music, Sand Sculpting Demonstrations and hands on Lessons. The Kid's Zone is a place for the kids to practice their sand sculpting skills and get some hands on lessons. You don't want to miss this spectacular display of unbelievable works of art made from sand and water by some of the worlds top sand sculptors.

Back Roads Lodging - The Fort Gratiot Light Station includes a newly renovated duplex, that is available for overnight rental. The lodging program is designed to accommodate groups, and includes a tour, an explanation of the history of the light, and a description of future plans. The duplex is a modern facility. To reserve the duplex, contact the museum.

www.phmuseum.org – 810-982-0891

Sault Ste. Marie Getaway

Sault Ste. Marie means, "the Rapids of Saint Mary", in French. The Saint Mary's River connects Lake Superior to Lake Huron, and it is along the banks, and on the river, that visitors find much of what makes a getaway here so special. No matter what brings people to the "Soo", the sight of 1,000 foot long Great Lakes freighters, called "lakers", making their way through the locks, will be a lasting memory. The Soo Locks are a major attraction and the river is just a block from Portage Avenue, but there is a lot more to see and do.

Another feature of downtown Sault Ste. Marie is the distinctive architecture. The Chippewa County Historical Society History Center is housed in an 1899 building, that originally housed the Sault Ste. Marie News. Next to that, corner of Ashmun Street and Portage Avenue, is Island Books & Crafts. This is another historic building, that was the Sault Savings Bank, and that housed the Traverse Bay Woolen Company. Then there is Cloverland Electric Cooperative's, historic hydroelectric plant. The building is impossible to miss, it's nearly a quarter mile long, and has been in operation for over 100 years. It is the longest, horizontal shaft, hydroelectric plant in the world, and has been in operation since 1902. The Chippewa County Court House building has to be seen to be appreciated. We just don't build them like this anymore.

Day 1 - Around Town - In addition to the historic buildings, there are shops, museums, and parks, along Portage Ave. A visit to the Tower of History involves an elevator ride, up 200+ feet, to an observation deck. The view of Sault Ste. Marie, the river, the locks, and Canada is unmatched anywhere. The S.S. Valley Camp is a retired ore freighter, at a permanent dock, that now serves as a museum ship. Exhibits inside the ship focus on the maritime heritage of the "Soo". While exploring the ship, visitors will find two lifeboats from the wreck of the SS Edmund Fitzgerald. These are the only major Edmund Fitzgerald artifacts ever recovered.

Just a couple of blocks off Portage Ave, up Ashmun St., is the River of History Museum. The museum preserves the thousands of years of the history of this region. The exhibits tell the story of this region, the St. Mary River, and the founding of Sault Ste. Marie in 1668, the first European settlement in Michigan. The narrative at the museum begins with the glaciers receding. Then the stories of the first people, the fur trade, the Anishinabeg and French Voyageurs, and onward to the French claiming the land, the establishment of the Michigan Territory, and more.

Day 2 - Road Trips - 20 miles east of Sault Ste. Marie, along the Whitefish Bay Scenic Byway, is the Point Iroquois Light Station. It can be a day trip by itself, or a stop, on the scenic drive to Tahquamenon Falls. You can climb to the top of the light for a panoramic view of Lake

Superior and Point Iroquois. The on site museum exhibits lightkeeper family albums and artifacts, from the times when the light was a critical navigational aid to traffic, on Whitefish Bay.

Lighthouse enthusiasts actually don't even have to leave town. Located next to the Coast Guard Station, on historic Water Street, is the *Frying Pan Island Lighthouse*. The stubby, white lighthouse can be easily seen from the street or sidewalk. The lighthouse was constructed in 1887, and was originally located in the De Tour Passage on Frying Pan Island.

Perhaps the most photographed waterfall in the upper peninsula, *Tahquamenon Falls*, remains a favorite day trip, in summer and winter. The fast way to get there from Sault Ste. Marie, is south on I-75 to Route 28, then west to Route 123, and then north to the Tahquamenon Falls State Park. The scenic route to the falls, is west on 6 Mile Road, which becomes Lakeshore Drive. That road will become the Lake Superior Lakeshore Drive, with great views of the lake. Stay on Lakeshore Dr. to Route 123, and then, go north. At Tahquamenon, there are upper and lower falls, separated by forest, but connected by hiking trails. The upper falls is about 200 feet across and has a drop of nearly 50 feet. It is an unforgetable scene when parts of it freeze in winter. The lower falls is a series of cascades and is much more interactive. Both falls exhibit a distinctive red color from the tannins of the leaves in the water. A State Park passport is required.

Day 3 - Nature Areas - This entire area, is surrounded by the Hiawatha National Forest, so nature areas abound. Sault Ste. Marie has a number of close in nature venues, so once again, you don't even have to leave town to get back to nature. *Brady Park* is close to downtown on the site of the original Fort Brady. Locals and visitors gather to watch the giant "lakers" on the river. There are huge maple trees and extensive flower beds. In addition to the informative displays about early history, there is a "Torii" This is a unique archway, designed in the Japanese tradition. At night, the fountain is lighted and choreographed to music.

The Sault Seal Recreation Area, locally known as Minneapolis Woods, is a major site for winter activities. There is a large hill, with a great view, that is equipped with several snow tubing runs. On the other side of the hill is a network of walking trails known as *Lynn Trails*. They are suitable for cross country skiing, but are also excellent for a nature walk in the warm months. One part of the trail takes you along a wetland on a 200 foot long boardwalk. The recreation area is at the end East 20th, south of town, off Ashmun St.

Then there is the treasure in the river. To the southeast of downtown, are several islands, in the St. Mary's River. At one time they were referred to as island 1, island 2, etc. Now with the development of *Voyageur Island Park*, the islands all have names. To reach the islands, you will have to paddle out in a canoe, kayak, or other boat.

Paddlers can head out from Rotary Island Park or Harvey Marina. After crossing the Riverside Channel, it only takes a few minutes, boaters can choose a shore landing, or the new Paddler Dock. Once on the island, well maintained hiking trails are waiting. There is the Riverside Trail, that leads to a boardwalk and observation platform. The Ridge Trail runs through diverse habitats before connecting with the other trails. Then there is the very popular *Freighter Trail*. This trail runs along the shipping channel, affording up close views of the enormous Great Lakes freighters heading to and from the famous Soo Locks.

Winter Fun - The nearby trails and parks, are great for cross country skiing and snowshoe hiking. If you plan your trip for the right time of year, Sault Ste. Marie is the home of the International 500 Snowmobile Race, known as the I-500. Contestants from all over the U.S. and Canada, have been coming to Sault Ste. Marie every year since 1969. Powerful snowmobiles roar around a frozen track, at over 100 miles per hour, to the delight of one and all. The race takes place on the only 1-mile oval ice track in North America. The action on the banked turns is unbelievable.

A Bit of History - The *Engineers Day Festival* is one event that should be on your bucket list. On one day only each year, visitors can walk across the Soo Locks walls and tour the buildings and exhibits available on this day only, the last Friday in June.

Part of *Engineers Day* is the tour of the *Cloverland Electric Cooperative Hydroelectric Plant*. This building, at a quarter mile long, can't be missed, and on this day only, visitors can go inside. The plant is 80 feet wide and has seventy-four horizontal shaft turbines located on the generation floor level. Each turbine has four runners (blades). The water, flowing down the power canal, drops through gates in the turbines to make them spin. The turbine turns the rotor—the last moving part. The turning creates electricity. Amazingly, half of the original wood bearings for the turbines are still in use. The bearings were made from lignum vitae, a rare wood of very high density, found in Central and South America.

Back Roads Lodging - A wide variety of lodging choices are available in Sault Ste. Marie. For lodging information, and details about the attractions in town, contact the Convention & Visitors Bureau 225 E. Portage Ave.

www.saultstemarie.com - 906-632-3366

Sleeping Bear Dune Getaway

The Sleeping Bear Dunes National Lakeshore has something to offer everyone, a 72,000 acre park, with boating and canoeing, hiking, scenic beauty, fishing and wildlife, and miles of pristine beaches. Dune climbs are there for those in good shape and boardwalks make it all accessible, to the rest of us. In spite of the thousands of visitors, there are plenty of hiking opportunities, that lead into wilderness areas, that contain only the sounds of nature.

The famous dunes are only a small part of this region. There are rivers to float, trails to hike, scenic drives to enjoy, and unique historic destinations. Port Oneida is one of the best preserved, historic agricultural districts, in America. The Platte River has become famous for water sports, including excellent salmon fishing.

Day 1 - Sleeping Bear Dunes - The dunes are the most famous attraction in the area. They are living dunes, with constant movement and changes. About 200 acres of Sleeping Bear Point, disappeared in 1915, as the dunes moved about six feet a year, burying everything in their path. There are cedar trees here, that were growing when Europeans first arrived. There are glacial formations, that are older than the pyramids, and there are vistas, from hundreds of feet above Lake Michigan, providing views of those stunning sunsets.

Day 2 - Two Scenic Drives - The Port Oneida Historic Area - Pierce Stocking Drive

Port Oneida is one of the most unique historic districts, in all of Michigan. Located within the borders of the Sleeping Bear National Lakeshore, it is one of the least visited attractions, in the entire area. Perhaps that is because it doesn't appear on the Michigan map. Empire is shown, as is Pyramid Point, but not Port Oneida. When you get to Empire, make a quick stop at the ranger station. Pick up the Port Oneida booklet, that has descriptions of the buildings, and a simple map. You'll need the map to find your way around the district. Port Oneida grew into a sizable community in the late 1800s, as a result of the lumber industry, and the work of Thomas Kelderhouse. Eventually, the area included a dock on Lake Michigan, blacksmith shop, post office, general store, and a boarding house.

When the trees were gone, the dock and mill were closed. By 1908, all of the buildings of the original town site, except the Kelderhouse residence, had been abandoned. A number of small farms continued to struggle for existence. Most were no longer farmed after World War II.

The trip through the Port Oneida Historic District, can be enjoyed by car or bicycle. Note that some of these farms are on gravel roads. The tour meanders through the agricultural area of Pyramid Point, and takes you to 10 -

15 farmsteads, and the old Port Oneida schoolhouse. The Charles Olsen Farm is one of the first stops you will come to. The office for Preserve Historic Sleeping Bear is located at this farm and, if open, is a good source for additional information. While you go from farm to farm, you will also come across the Kelderhouse Cemetery, and the farm next to it. The present house has also been used as a grocery store, telephone exchange, and post office. Some of the barns are worth visiting, like the Miller Barn. There is old machinery scattered around, and some of the barns still have huge field stones as part of their foundations. Most of the buildings are well preserved, and visitors are encouraged to wander around. Some, like the Weaver Farm, are badly weathered, and in poor condition.

One of the most photographed barns in Michigan, on the *D. H. Day* farmstead, is nearby. The barn, built in the late 1800s, has twin silos and an ogee (bell-shaped) roof, with octagonal cupolas topping it all off. You really can't miss it. It doesn't lie in the historic district but is within the boundaries of the park.

The Bay View Hiking Trail also runs through the district and offers a convenient way to see some of the more remote parts of the district. Whether driving, biking, or hiking, it is not unusual to spend a couple of hours here and only see one or two other people. You can really enjoy the quiet and isolation of these beautiful farmlands. The *Pierce Stocking Scenic Drive*, a legacy from the lumberman Pierce Stocking, is a scenic route, within Sleeping Bear Dunes National Lakeshore. This drive, and the surrounding area, have been called the most beautiful place in America. The drive is just a bit more than 7 miles in length and is open in the summer months only. Those 7 miles offer up some of the most beautiful over-looks in Michigan. The roadway, with its amazing vistas, is located off state highway M-109 between Empire and Glen Arbor.

The covered bridge is one of the first features encountered. A pull off is provided, as this is a favorite spot for photography. There are several scenic turn offs and picnic areas. Spectacular views of Lake Michigan, the Manitou Islands, and the Sleeping Bear Dune are found all along the way. The scenes, from atop the 400+ foot high dunes, really can be described as breathtaking. Another view is of Glen Lake, connected to Lake Michigan during the Ice Age, it is known for its remarkably blue waters. Hiking trails lead into the forests, but even staying on the road, will bring you to trees that are hundreds of years old. Dune climbers flock here, to take on the challenge, of some of the highest and steepest dunes in the area. The sunsets are so beautiful that many folks bring a picnic along to just enjoy the onset of evening.

Day 3 - Float The River - There is no end to the fun you can have on the water in this area, from rock hunting on the shore, to floating the *Platte River*. The Platte River is

10 miles south of Empire, at the junction with Lake Michigan Road and M-22. This river is a favorite for kayaking, canoeing, and tubing. This is a fun float, that is enjoyable for all ages, and skill levels. The river meanders through woodlands at a gentle pace. There are a few small rapids, and a few places to pull off to take a refreshing swim in the sparkling waters.

At some seasons of the year, the salmon will be running the river, attracting fishermen from across the nation. At those times, don't be surprised to see schools of salmon navigating the river, right underneath your tube or paddle board. After a leisurely drift, you arrive at Lake Michigan. There is a nice park here, and a beach that winds around to some great places for rock collecting. Almost every evening, stunning sunsets are served up free, for all to enjoy from this same park. You can get to the beach without floating the river, by following Lake Michigan Road west from M-22.

Winter Fun - The *Old Indian Trail* is accessible from the main road M-109. There is a place to park right at the trail head. Though it is listed here under winter fun, this trail is great fun in every season. The terrain is mostly flat and straight, with some gentle hills and small curves, making the going easy, even for beginning cross country skiers. However, on the advanced loop, there is a downhill run that is rather steep. Eventually, after meandering through the pine and oak trees of the forest, the trail serves up a lovely view of Lake Michigan, and the famous sand dunes. This beautiful coastal lowland was under water thousands of years ago, so the vegetation varies. There are even a few hemlock trees found here.

Along The Way - Almost any turn-off, from the main road M-22, will lead to the gorgeous beaches of Lake Michigan, with the Manitou Islands shimmering in the distance. If the side road doesn't lead to a beach, it will probably lead to a small lake, new hiking trails or a secret fishing spot. It is worth the effort to check them all, though many seem to be just gravel tracks, leading into the forest. Three days is not enough time, so plan to return again and again.

Back Roads Lodging - *The Empire Lakeshore Inn,* at the northwest corner of M-22 and M-72, is centrally located for your explorations. Street address: 11730 S. Lacore Road, Empire, MI.

www.empirelakeshoreinn.net – 231-326-5145

St. Ignace Getaway

St. Ignace, the second oldest settlement in Michigan, lies at the northern end of the Mackinac Bridge. The picturesque downtown boasts unique shops, restaurants specializing in local recipes, and historical museums, all strung along the waterfront on Lake Huron. Shimmering in the distance, across the bay, is the famous Mackinac Island, a favorite destination for a day trip.

St. Ignace is unique for its woods, its waters, and its history. The Hiawatha National Forest surrounds the entire region. Within the forest, are scenic trails, spectacular waterfalls, and hundreds of lakes and rivers, to explore. Historic treasures lie beneath the sparkling waters. The Great Lakes Shipwreck Preserve is home to some of the best preserved shipwrecks in the world. Wrecks from the 1800s through the 1960s await divers. There are three sites accessible from the shores of St. Ignace. Local history is told through several museums and memorials, like the Father Marquette National Memorial.

Day 1 - Explore Downtown - Huron Boardwalk - Pavillion Shops - Mysterious Newberry Tablets

The *Huron Boardwalk* follows the curve of the bay, giving access to all of the attractions downtown, as well as parks, multiple beaches, and marinas. The boardwalk features open air exhibits, and interpretive stations, describing the history, colorful characters, and natives who inhabited the Straits of Mackinac, and built St. Ignace. During warm weather, a stop at Molly Moos for ice cream is a good idea, and the Mackinac Grille is a favorite for planked whitefish.

Shops line State Street offering souvenirs and local crafts. The *Pavillion* is exceptional, in all of northern Michigan, with it's half dozen shops, bakery, and wine shop. On Tuesday evenings visitors gather for a *wine tasting*.

Several museums are downtown, each with a gift shop. The Fort De Buade Museum has an extensive gift shop and is the home of the enigmatic *Newberry Stones*.

In 1896, a tremendous wind storm swept across the upper peninsula. One of the trees the storm blew over, was on the farm of John McGuer. According to the Soo Evening News, several mysterious objects were stuck in the root system of an enormous old hemlock, felled by that storm. The items included 3 statues and a large stone tablet. The tablet was engraved with strange inscriptions.

The largest statue was nearly life size and seems to depict a man sitting on a sort of pedestal. The second appeared to be a woman and is a bit smaller. The third, and smallest statue, seems to be the image of a child. All three are of sandstone and have the appearance of great age. The tablet, found nearby, was about 18" by 25". One side was covered with 140 inscriptions, engraved in rows. Each row was made up of squares about 1 ½ inches in size. Some have interpreted the inscriptions as Minoan. No one has been able to determine the actual origin of the objects, or how they made it to Michigan. The McGruer statues and the Newberry Tablet are on display at the *Fort De Buade Museum.* The original newspaper articles and photographs are there as well.

Day 2 - Local Attractions - Mackinac Bridge - Castle Rock - 16 Lighthouses

The *Mackinac Bridge* was heralded as one of the great engineering feats of the time. It still stands as a definitive icon of the upper peninsula of Michigan. The bridge is the scene of a number of events each year, including the annual Bridge Walk.

Castle Rock is considered to be one of the oldest lookout points near the city of St. Ignace, and was known as "Pontiac's Lookout", by the Ojibwa Tribe. Clarence Eby opened Castle Rock for tourists in 1929. It has remained a popular destination ever since. The "Rock" rises an astonishing 195 feet above water level, and about 183 feet above I-75. Visitors who climb "the rock" are rewarded with a view of the entire surrounding area. A view that is unmatched anywhere. The summit of Castle Rock offers a scenic and inspiring view for up to 20 miles, featuring Mackinac Island, Lake Huron, downtown St. Ignace, and the surrounding forests. The lookout point is equipped with viewing binoculars, for a truly spectacular view of the area. This is one attraction that is family friendly, pet friendly, and, and not be missed.

There are a number of water based attractions here, including a tour of *16 Lighthouses*. Most of the lighthouses can be seen from shore, but the best way to get close is by taking one of the tours, offered by the local cruise companies. Another bonus of these cruises is going under the Mackinac Bridge.

Day 3 - Scenic Drives - Tahquamenon Falls - Mackinac Trail Drive - Crisp Point Lighthouse - Lake Michigan Shore

Perhaps the most photographed waterfall in the upper peninsula, *Tahquamenon Falls*, remains a favorite day trip, in summer and winter. The drive up Route 123 winds through great pine forests. There are upper and lower falls, separated by forest, but connected by hiking trails. The upper falls is about 200 feet across and has a drop of nearly 50 feet. It is an amazing scene when parts of it freeze in winter. The lower falls is a series of cascades. There are trails and boardwalks through the lower falls. Both falls exhibit a distinctive red color from the tannins of the leaves in the water.

Another short scenic drive is old Route H-63. Locally called Mackinac Trail, it is reached by heading north on State Street. Just before you get to Castle Rock is the sign. It is a two lane paved road that runs parallel to I-75. You will ride through tall pines and cross sparkling streams. On the way is Fort Algonquin, one of the last original tourist traps left. In just a few miles, the road intersects with Route 123, the route to the Tahquamenon Falls.

The most remote lighthouse in Michigan, is within driving distance. ***Crisp Point Lighthouse*** is far up on the shore of Lake Superior. It will take most of a day but is at an incredibly beautiful spot. The best route is to go north, out of Newberry, to Route H-37 to Pine Stump Junction. From there it is all rough gravel roads. Follow the signs. If you rely on a GPS device, you may end up on roads that can be impassible. Despite the gravel, this is one of the best day trips in the eastern upper peninsula.

Route 2 is the main highway going west, along the ***Lake Michigan Shore***, with views of lighthouses, islands, and soaring sand dunes. On the drive, you can stop at Wildwood for pasties, or a slice of their famous Mile High Apple Pie. In October and November they even make venison pasties. After a little over 40 miles, you will reach Naubinway, and the ***Top of the Lake Snowmobile Museum***. The museum has more than 80 vintage sleds of all kinds. Some are from the 1950s, and some are old prototypes, for racing sleds. Driving north out of Naubinway will get you to Route H-40. Turn east and enjoy the drive back to Route 123, and back to St. Ignace.

Winter Fun - Pond Hockey - Ice Bridge

The largest adult ***pond hockey tournament*** in Michigan, takes place in St. Ignace in February. It is the only tourney that is played on one of the Great Lakes. The event is fun for all, and has hosted more than 150 teams, from around the world. Another winter event in St. Ignace is the formation of the *"ice bridge"*. While most businesses on Mackinac Island are closed in winter, some do remain open. When the bay freezes, a route is marked out with Christmas trees, to define a safe passage to the island, for snowmobiles. Though the "bridge" is frozen, there can be thin ice, and open water just a few feet away.

Along The Way - St. Ignace, Michigan is one of the oldest settlements in the state. Within view of the "Bridge" is the Father Marquette Memorial, honoring the missionary, who came here in the 1600s. Festivals are a part of life year round with Fish Feast in July, History Week in August, and the Tractor Parade in September, just to name a few.

Back Roads Lodging
The historic *Colonial House Inn B&B*
www.colonial-house-inn.com - 906-643-6900

The modern *Cedar Hill Lodge*
www.cedarhilllodge.com
906-643-9900

Timber Ridge Getaway

Grand Traverse County, in Northern Michigan, is best known for it's most famous town, Traverse City. Front Street and downtown Traverse City are popular destinations, but there is a lot more to see in this region. This getaway is based out of the *Timber Ridge Resort,* an RV and Recreation Resort. However, you don't have to own a camper to take advantage of their hospitality and amenities. The resort offers year round cabins, yurts, and really cool vintage trailers for rent.

Since the resort is just eight miles from the crowds in downtown Traverse City, it is an ideal location from which to explore. It is easy to get to some of the lesser known destinations and attractions in the area and enjoy Front Street and the Grand Traverse Bay as well. There is history to discover, rare music, pristine nature and a couple of places that are mostly known to the locals only.

Day 1 – The Resort - In addition to the lodging, the resort offers amenities that may just keep you there the whole time. They have a heated pool, several varieties of ball courts, wooded hiking, biking, and motor sport trails immediately adjacent to the property. You don't even need to bring your bike with you, they have fat tire bikes and electric cargo bikes for rent. Biking is one of the most popular activities in the north. In fact, some people gather here just to watch the Iceman Cometh racers. They go ripping by every November on the *VASA Trail* that borders the resort. This is a great place to work on your snowshoe muscles, as well. If all of that isn't enough, the Grand Traverse region is right outside the gates with something for everyone.

Day 2 – Rare History – There are so many attractions near the resort that it is easy to overlook two of the most unique. Both would be standout destinations anywhere int the mid-west. One is the Music House Museum. As is often the case, the name doesn't give much of a clue to the treasures inside the museum, which features, "Restored musical instruments from the late 18th century in a converted granary & barn." The tour is essential to understanding the incredible variety of items on display. Here are a few of the most remarkable.

There are several pianos including a Conover Cable Grand Piano. The one on display is a prototype. These were built upright because rooms were small. This style went out of favor because rooms in modern homes don't have 9 foot ceilings. Then there is a Reproducing Piano from 1925. This piano was used before the invention of recording microphones. Music is recorded while being played on a 5' canister roll, this one is valued at about $10,000.

The crown jewel of the museum is their Belgian Mortier Dance Organ, known as the "Amaryllis". There were about 1,400 of these constructed. The "Amaryllis" was built for the Victorian Palace Dance Hall in Belgium. It is more than 30 feet wide and 18 feet high. There are only 24 of these giant music machines still in extant. The organ is entirely mechanical, no electric motors, and runs via a hand crafted flywheel. A man stood behind the facade and cranked the wheel at a very specific speed to create the correct music. Each organ had a unique music book of songs. The songs would be the same, but the coding would be different. The upshot was that book would only work on the organ it was created for. Owners were unable to swap or loan the music book.

Sometimes a rise to world fame has very humble beginnings; and so it was for Colantha Walker, *the wonder cow*. The Northern Michigan Asylum opened in 1885 and eventually grew into a giant complex on the outskirts of Traverse City, Michigan. In fact, at one point the population of the hospital complex, 3,500, was greater than the population of the city at that time. The Asylum was self-sufficient with its own farms, gardens, fire department and power plant. It had its own orchards of peaches, apples and cherries, its own vineyards and vegetable gardens, field crops and a wide variety of livestock including a herd of cows.

The most famous of these, actually the most famous inhabitant of the asylum period, was Colantha Walker, a grand champion milk cow. In her long and storied career - from 1916 to 1932 - she produced 200,114 pounds of milk and 7,525 pounds of butterfat. In her best year, 1926, her annual production was a world record 22,918 pounds of milk. The official state average was 3,918 pounds.

When Colantha went to her reward in 1932, the staff and patients of the asylum held a banquet in her honor and erected a huge granite tombstone over her grave. The *Tomb of the Cow* is tucked away on the south edge of the property near the old original barns. At a curve in the road just south of two champion Black Willows, the engraved stone sits between two trees. She is the only resident of the asylum to be buried on the grounds. The asylum has been transformed into the Commons. It contains offices, shops and condominiums.

Day 3 – Local Nature Areas – Highbanks Roll Away – Miller Creek Preserve

There are several trails to enjoy at Timber Ridge and the entire resort is like a big nature area. Among all of the other nature areas nearby, two are favorites of locals and travelers in the know.

Little known and spectacular is the *High Banks Roll-Away*. One stretch of the Manistee River provides some of the most pristine river scenes and experiences anywhere in Michigan. The Highbanks Roll Away may be the most beautiful overlook in lower Michigan. This is one of those landmarks with no "official" name. It is known variously as, Horseshoe Bend Overlook, Lookout Point or the Highbanks Overlook. When you stand at the top, the scenery is beyond description. It easily compares to the Lake of the Clouds or the Snow Bowl overlook. From the lookout it's 200 - 300 feet down to the river. The valley below unfolds like a gigantic bowl revealing more than 100 square miles of dense pine and hardwood forest. The distant horizon runs roughly from Manton in the east, around to Meauwataka and Harrietta in the south and west to Mesick.

The Horseshoe Bend is a favorite destination on the river. This part of the river is a perfect choice for tubing and kayaking. The river and trails wind through pines and hardwoods, wetlands and valleys. Every kind of northern Michigan wildlife abounds. When you get down to the dam, you can pause and watch the eagles fly. A float trip will also bring you to two unique bridges: an arch timber bridge crossing Slagle Creek and a suspension bridge over the Manistee River linking the north end of the trail with the Marilla segment of the *North Country Trail,* on the west side of the river. Rollways were used to stock logs along the river bank and later during the spring thaw, roll them into the water for floating.

When asking about cool walking trails in the area, locals will often mention the **Miller Creek Preserve Trail** as a favorite. It may seem unlikely, but the trail is hidden away behind the Walmart and Crossings Mall. There is good parking and you walk out of the city and into the wilderness. The trails pass through a former red pine plantation, skirt the edges of open meadows, wind through beautiful beech forests, cross boardwalks through cedar swamps, and follow Miller Creek, a tributary of the Boardman River. The whole 60+ acre Miller Creek Nature Reserve is beautiful. Recreational opportunities at this park include hiking, nature watching, hunting (with prior Township approval), cross country skiing, and snowshoeing. There are two trailheads, both of which are located behind the Crossings Mall. The southern entrance is behind Office Depot; the other is off of Crossing Circle Drive, near Faith Reformed Church. The trails can also be accessed from the northwest corner of the former Sabin Elementary School property at the intersection of Hartman and Cass Roads.

Along The Way – The variety of dining options in Grand Traverse County can be overwhelming. If you are looking for a place that is so good it has lasted more than 100 years, try *Sleder's Family Tavern*. This legendary saloon features pub grub and drinks in a rustic interior festooned with taxidermy. Sleder's has been in business since 1882. To put that in perspective, that is just 5 years after George Armstrong Custer made that error in judgment out on the Little Big Horn. They say the bar is the original from the 1800s. Sleder's is at 717 Randolph St, Traverse City, MI 49684

Timber Ridge Resort
4050 Hammond Road E. (From East 31 take 5 Mile Rd)
Traverse City, MI. 49686
Phone: (231) 947-2770

Notes

Notes

Notes

Notes